The National Environmental Policy Act

NUMBER SEVENTEEN
Environmental History Series
Dan Flores, General Editor

The National Environmental Policy Act

Judicial Misconstruction, Legislative Indifference, & Executive Neglect

MATTHEW J. LINDSTROM & ZACHARY A. SMITH

Foreword by Lynton K. Caldwell

TEXAS A&M UNIVERSITY PRESS • COLLEGE STATION

Library fo Congress Cataloging-in-Publication Data

Lindstrom, Matthew J., 1969–
      The national environmental policy act : judicial misconstruction,
  legislative indifference, and executive neglect / Matthew J. Lindstrom
  and Zachary A. Smith ; foreword by Lynton K. Caldwell.—1st ed.
          p. cm.—(Environmental history series ; no. 17)
      Includes bibliographical references and index.
      ISBN 1-58544-125-2
          1. Environmental policy—United States—History—20th century.
  2. United States. National Environmental Policy Act of 1969.
  I. Smith, Zachary A. (Zachary Alden), 1953–   II. Title.   III. Series.
  GE180.L55   2001
  363.7'056'0973—dc21   2001002410

CONTENTS

FOREWORD

It has now been over thirty years since President Richard Nixon signed the National Environmental Policy Act (NEPA) into law on January 1, 1970, and there has long been need for a comprehensive and detailed account of this statute, its origin, influence, and implementation. In 1989, I complained—as authors Lindstrom and Smith have noted—that "there never has been a thorough and objective account about the evolution of this extraordinary act." With this book, there now is.

Some lapse of time was necessary before the history of this act could be written. NEPA was enacted with bipartisan support at a critical point in the nation's history. It is doubtful whether NEPA could have been enacted before or after the several years during which it was drafted. Comparable legislation between 1959 and 1969 failed to obtain Congressional attention. However, in the years preceding 1969, a series of widely publicized environmental disasters aroused popular concern and a demand that the federal government "do something" to prevent future occurrences of similar events. What was done is the substance of this book.

During the years from 1965 to 1975, popular concern in the United States and Western Europe over the state of the land, air, water, and wildlife—for which the inclusive term "the environment" is used—became conventional in political discourse. Before this period, environmental concerns were customarily perceived as natural resources issues.

After 1970, as the environment started being differentiated from natural resources, it was widely perceived as relating almost exclusively to pollution of air and water. When NEPA was signed into law, the *New York Times* and the *Washington Post,* usually knowledgeable about public affairs, announced that Nixon's anti-pollution law was enacted. And subsequently, in these newspapers the appointees to the Council of Environmental Quality were described as "Nixon's pollution fighters."

In retrospect, it appears that many members of Congress had the same perception. But no congressman in 1969 wanted to face his constituents as a protector of unconscionable polluters. The farming and business communities, and notably the real estate developers and builders, were awakened to the broad scope of NEPA when Senator Henry Jackson introduced the National Land Use Policy Act of 1970 as the logical sequel to NEPA. The ensuing polarization of political parties on environmental policy issues, although never uniform among party activists, grew over the years to become opposing tendencies in the two major political parties.

My published writings on NEPA from 1963 to 1973 have been brought together in the book *Environment as a Focus for Public Policy*, edited by Robert V. Bartlett and James N. Gladden, published in 1995 by the Texas A&M University Press, and selected as a *Choice* recommended book by the American Library Association. As shown in these writings, I have been closely involved in the implementation of NEPA. Too close, it appears, to be regarded as an objective witness. Fortunately, Matthew Lindstrom and Zachary Smith have given us the history that we have needed.

If a sustainable future is a national goal, then NEPA sets the standards for public decision making and action. This is a book useful not only in comprehending the underutilized potential of NEPA, but also as a basic reference book on environmental policy in the United States and, generally, in the rest of the world as well. After all, a joint CEQ–Department of State survey found influence of the Act in at least eighty countries worldwide. This survey clearly demonstrates that NEPA has been the most widely emulated statute ever enacted by the U.S. Congress.

Lynton K. Caldwell

This book is written with the hope that public opinion and our political institutions of all sizes can recognize the vital need for sustainable economies and environmental stewardship. As we pass into a new century and a new millennium, the time is ripe to explore the values and policy visions that will help our planet and all its inhabitants live in greater harmony. It is our belief that the U.S. National Environmental Policy Act of 1969 (NEPA) offers the environmental ethics as well as the administrative tools for realizing such ecological goals, while balancing these with our other national needs. If current economic and societal pressures upon the environment continue to grow, NEPA's substantive and procedural policy values and mechanisms will be ever more salient.

NEPA did not appear in a vacuum. Rather, it was a congressional response to widespread public concern during the mid- to late 1960s regarding environmental degradation and the demand that Congress "do something" to "fix the problem." Clearly, the passage and implementation of NEPA have vastly improved and coordinated the federal government's processes regarding the natural environment, a vital step toward escaping the quagmires of ecological policy disputes and inadequacies. Unlike any other statute, NEPA provides the most appropriate framework within which federal agencies can treat the environment, because it lays down a broad set of ecological goals and legislates a holistic, cautionary, and preventive method for arriving at federal decisions and actions regarding our natural environment. By creating and passing NEPA, "Congress recognized that nearly all federal activities affect the environment in some way, and realize that before federal agencies make decisions, they must consider the effects of their actions on the quality of the human environment."[1]

Signed by President Richard Nixon on January 1, 1970, NEPA is Public Law 91-190. Prior to NEPA, each federal agency had an ad hoc environmental policy—if it had any policy at all. This piecemeal approach was not only organizationally and fiscally inefficient, it also grossly neglected the interconnectedness of the natural world and the benefits of coordinating policy making. NEPA's authors, motivated by the natural sciences and by public concern, recognized this lack of coordination and wrote a set of policy goals and procedural tools that required an integrated analysis of environmental impacts created by federal actions.

However, despite the fact that NEPA is "real law" and not an inconsequential congressional resolution without teeth, the federal courts, and above all the Supreme Court, have rendered the core values expressed in NEPA's preamble and Title I to be void of enforceable ecological mandates. Therefore, the commitment of federal agencies toward NEPA's values and visions has been quite mixed. On the one hand, the environmental impact statement, created by Title I, is procedurally enforceable. But it has not been used consistently to implement the act's ecological goals. The requirement that an environmental impact statement be written has generated widespread litigation around federal projects—some successful in forcing compliance with NEPA's goals. Moreover, U.S. states and many other countries have copied NEPA's environmental impact procedure, which further exemplifies the importance and success of the law.

It is the thesis of this book that NEPA has had a positive impact on environmental policy in the United States and on the quality of American life in general. However, it is also our contention (shared by others) that the substantive ethics, principles, and goals declared in NEPA's section 101 are regularly treated by federal courts and agencies as nothing more than wishful thinking having no practical effect or importance for federal agency decisions and actions. The divergence between enforcing the procedural actions required by NEPA and meeting its substantial policy values is a central issue we explore throughout this book.

To address this split between implementing the required actions or procedures but not the values and goals behind the procedures, we offer a detailed history of NEPA's legislative origins, its place and effects within environmental law, and its implementation and enforcement by federal agencies and courts. In essence, we trace how and why the law was created (chaps. 1 and 2), what the law's goals are (chap. 3), how it is being implemented (chaps. 4 and 5), and how its implementation and enforcement have fallen short of its authors' intentions (chaps. 6 and 7). Finally, we discuss NEPA's unrealized potential for carrying not only this country but also the whole world into a sustainable, ecologically conscious twenty-first century (chap. 7).

Because our work here is both historical and contemporary, and examines policy, administrative, and legal ramifications of the law, we believe it will be of interest to a wide array of people. Insofar as this book offers a historical and contemporary analysis of federal policy, politics, and administration with respect to NEPA, it can be useful for federal and other government agencies, all sorts of interest groups concerned about environmental issues, and students and scholars in the fields of public administration, political science, and environmental studies. Students of environmental history, particularly the history of environmental law, may find our presentation of NEPA's legislative evolution useful by itself or in a comparative setting. Practitioners and academics who work in the area of environment policy, especially impact analysis, are provided with a discussion of NEPA from its prelegislative beginnings through the vices and virtues of its implementation and on to its potential in the twenty-first century.

There are no quick or easy solutions for executing environmental goals, and NEPA is no exception. But it is our belief that NEPA provides one of the clearest and most logical road maps to a world where our society's environmental, economic, social, and cultural goals do not collide but are instead seen as fundamentally interdependent and mutually beneficial for all Earth's creatures, human and nonhuman.

ACKNOWLEDGMENTS

It took many years and much help for us to finish this book. Northern Arizona University (NAU) provided us with a solid group of environmental policy scholars with which to work. Matt's current employer Siena College, located in New York's Capital District, is another reason we were able to complete this book. Susan Kuebler of Siena College tirelessly worked on frequent revisions to the book manuscript. The staff at Siena's Standish Library provided Matt with comfortable research space and timely document retrieval services. The Siena College Committee on Teaching's faculty research grants and the Office of Institutional Planning and Research support allowed us the time to finish writing and researching final aspects of the book. Malcolm Willison did a very excellent job editing the manuscript. Indiana University professor Lynton K. Caldwell is a life-long source of inspiration for both of us and was instrumental in the formation of this book (and NEPA itself). Matt's extended family and children, Isaac and Anna, have patiently allowed him the time to do the necessary work to complete this book. Matt extends a special gratitude of thanks to his wife, Amy, who has encouraged him—since day one—to strive for excellence in all that he does. Whether or not excellence was achieved in this book is up to each individual reader. To those we named and to the many others we haven't named, we sincerely thank you.

The National Environmental Policy Act

CHAPTER I

The Values and Legislative Intent of the National Environmental Policy Act

In this book, we explain what a former Council of Environmental (CEQ) official called the "obliteration of substance in NEPA that has occurred in the courts and agency implementation."[1] Our central thesis is twofold. First, the National Environmental Policy Act (NEPA) sets forth a paradigm for making choices that sustain and enhance the quality and richness of human and nonhuman life. This paradigm could greatly contribute to furthering all forms of life in the twenty-first century. Second, NEPA's environmental impact statement (EIS) requirement (sec. 102) and the Council of Environmental Quality's 1978 regulations implementing this requirement are often more of a procedural paper chase than—as they were intended to be—a substantive vehicle for accurately assessing and mitigating the environmental impacts of proposed federal projects. We reach this conclusion by using the intent of NEPA's authors as a benchmark for evaluating NEPA's growth, development, and implementation. Dinah Bear, as former general counsel to the CEQ, stated: "The implementation of NEPA to date has been in some measure different from what the framers of the legislation anticipated."[2]

NEPA certainly was not, and is not, a panacea for national, much less global, environmental problems. However, through a close reading of the law's full text, its legislative history, and its implementing regulations issued by the Council of Environmental Quality, it is evident that NEPA was a considerable advance in public policy and still holds great utility as a model for environmental policy. This book hopes to support and enhance NEPA's influence on both counts.

NEPA is thought by many to be the natural environment's Magna Carta.[3] Substantively, NEPA's authors articulated historically unparalleled ecological goals for the federal government and the nation as a whole. Procedurally, the statute introduced a new tool into federal decision making, the environmental impact statement, a procedure intended to require that ecological principles and values be included in federal agency planning. NEPA represents one of the first attempts of any country at such a comprehensive law.

NEPA has two titles. Title I contains NEPA's purpose—a declaration of environmental policy—and mandates the consistent use of environmental impact statements. Title II establishes the Council on Environmental Quality in the executive office of the president. The passage of NEPA did three things: first, it declared a comprehensive national policy for the environment; second, it provided a new procedural tool for how federal agencies were to comply with the policy; third, by establishing the CEQ, it created an oversight mechanism to guide and supervise both the policy and its procedures. NEPA applies to all U.S. federal agencies and is supposed to apply to every agency action that significantly affects environmental quality. The immediate purpose of the law is to give federal agencies the statutory requirement and power to consider how their actions affect the natural environment and incorporate mitigating efforts. NEPA also requires federal agencies to establish communication with the public through open meetings and other avenues of comment. Although arguably the most pervasive, holistic, and important environmental law ever enacted, the understanding, application, and postpassage evolution of NEPA have so far shown only mixed success.

Indeed, while supported in theory by many constituencies, NEPA is mired in controversy over its implementation. Congressman James Hansen (R-Utah), as chair of the Resources Subcommittee on National Parks and Public Lands in the 106th Congress, stated that "NEPA simply serves as a tool of the bureaucrats to achieve desired results and predetermined decisions regardless of the public's input." In response to the Clinton administration's implementation of the law, Congressman Hansen added, "If the administration decides it wants a project to go forward, then it greases the process. If the administration decides it doesn't like a project, it crushes the process with paperwork—a paralysis of analysis that can take years and years and millions of dollars."[4]

Congressman Frank Pallone (D-N.J.), as a member of the Commerce Subcommittee on Health and Environment, while agreeing with Hansen's contention that NEPA could be improved, has maintained that "the act is arguably the most important of all environmental legislation." As we contend in this book, Pallone stated, "In many ways, NEPA was ahead of its time [in] advocating sustainable development before the term became fashionable. The act's shortcomings are not inherent in the statute itself. Rather they are a function of NEPA's implementation."[5]

This book traces NEPA's legal and political evolution, from formation to implementation to evaluation. Due to the law's importance as a template for ecological values and visions, as well as its effect on the procedures for federal planning, it is critical to analyze NEPA's legislative and legal history, contemporary effects, and future implications. In fact, Indiana University Emeritus Professor Lynton K. Caldwell, a primary architect of NEPA's policy statement and impact assessment requirement, noted the absence of any comprehensive approach to the act: "Unfortunately, there has never been a thorough and objective published account about the evolution of this extraordinary Act."[6] We attempt to address, in part at least, this void in the literature.

The purpose of this book is fourfold. First, we sketch evolution of the *concept* of environmental policy, from its roots in science, especially ecology, and the early conservation movement to contemporary interpretations. This task helps to establish the historical context in which NEPA was written and continues to be debated, implemented, and adjudicated. Why did the act's founders declare such a broad environmental policy? How did the framers understand the concepts of ecology and the environment?

The book's second component specifically addresses the statute's legislative history. To fully comprehend NEPA's potential to guide this country to better ecological choices, it is necessary to understand the law's historical and legislative context. Of central concern are the framers' intentions. Prior to its passage, the act was subject to thorough debate among legislators, President Richard Nixon's staff, and the consultants who helped draft the law. By ascertaining the law's pedigree, two important things become clear: first, Congress was navigating uncharted territory in constructing a national policy; second, the act was intended to institutionalize and enforce implementation of new environmental values and visions within the federal government.

Third, we examine the interpretation of NEPA by both the executive branch and the courts to show a pattern of only limited implementation and enforcement. We follow the labyrinthine path the federal courts have followed in ruling on NEPA's meaning and its legal mandates. Of related importance are the varying degree of seriousness federal agencies have toward NEPA's policy values and procedures, and the lackadaisical enforcement from the Supreme Court. Indeed, NEPA shook the very foundation of many agencies, which had heretofore never seriously considered ecological values nor envisioned or cared about the concept of sustainable development. These considerations were unrelated, or in some cases contrary, to the very mission of the agencies (e.g., the Bureau of Reclamation, Nuclear Regulatory Commission, Department of Commerce). The relationship between the courts and the executive branch is a very interesting one; at times each has pushed the other toward NEPA's environmental values, while at other times and in other contexts each branch has seemed to pull the other away from the core NEPA principles.

The fourth purpose of this book is to provide an assessment of NEPA's values and procedures and their interpretation in the context of today's environmental needs and politics. We hope to enlarge understanding of this unique and undervalued law. Not only has it revamped federal planning in the United States but also its design and principles continue to influence similar laws promulgated by U.S. states and by other governments and development agencies around the world. As several legal scholars contend, "[t]he rationality of this requirement—requiring documented formal consideration of negatives and alternatives as well as benefits before acting—may be obvious, but NEPA was its pioneer."[7]

To better understand and fully appreciate the breadth and depth of NEPA—its uniqueness, purpose, and future—several issues must be considered. First, as Caldwell has pointed out, NEPA is a policy act not a regulatory statute. Unlike most federal legislation, NEPA does not set concrete standards for emissions or cleanup requirements. The heart of NEPA is its declaration of environmental values for the country's public policy. NEPA, as a vision for national policy, should (and sometimes does) serve as a benchmark for gauging to what extent given decisions affecting the environment are supportive of NEPA's principles. Senator Henry Jackson, the chief NEPA sponsor in the Senate, emphasized the uniqueness of the act's visionary policy principles: "What is involved is a congressional declaration that we do not intend, as a government or as a people, to initiate actions which endanger the continued existence or the health of mankind [or] will do irreparable damage to the air [and] land. . ."[8]

These policy goals and values were very much reflected in the work of Caldwell—a "principle member of Senator Jackson's 'braintrust.'"[9] "The Ecosystem as a Criterion for Public Land Policy," his 1970 article published after the act passed in 1969, suggests that public policy, particularly land policy, incorporate ecological concepts within the discourse of natural resource planning. Professor Caldwell intended that this notion of a new ecological conscience be a fundamental part of NEPA's language and its interpretation.[10]

However, NEPA's framers did not naively believe the values and visions would be welcomed and endorsed by every federal agency. Therefore, NEPA includes several action-forcing provisions, including the EIS requirement and the establishment of the Council on Environmental Quality. The CEQ is charged with overseeing implementation of NEPA and periodically issues written guidance for federal agencies regarding the environmental impact assessment process and procedures. While CEQ does not have punative powers, the courts frequently use CEQ interpretations of NEPA in forming their decisions. The CEQ is also responsible for advising the president on environmental matters and annually reporting on the quality of the national environment.

The second point to understand about NEPA is that it sets more than a procedural requirement. The purpose of the act is to link the procedural provisions (sec. 102) with the declaration of values and vision (secs. 2 and 101). The linking of vision and values to the tools to ensure environmental sustainability is the heart and soul of the act. James McElfish and Elissa Parker summarize this linkage in *Rediscovering the National Environmental Policy Act:*

> The conventional wisdom about NEPA is that it is a flowery preamble attached to a single—and wholly procedural—requirement to prepare environmental impact statements for a small subset of federal decisions. This conventional wisdom is wrong. Like a classic of literature read when one is too young, what one remembers about NEPA is not, in fact, what

is most important about it. NEPA is not just an environmental impact statement law. It is rather, a vision of this nation's future, coupled with an intensely practical strategy for action."[11]

NEPA legislates values, not through a regulatory mandate but through a national declaration, and assists in the execution and incorporation of ecological values. In this regard, NEPA is unconventional in its purpose and design, which seek to reorganize the federal government's values and actions not through budgetary diversions or strict standards but by providing a set of goals and values for all agencies.

Third, NEPA's visions and procedures are not limited to a particular historical context or time frame. As we move into the twenty-first century, NEPA's principles become even more important as humans increasingly exploit and stress the environment in unsustainable ways. NEPA provides a way to harmonize economic priorities with other priorities necessary for clean, healthy, and just human communities.

The fact that NEPA creates a policy model that demands recognition of the environment's interconnectedness truly distinguishes it from other environmental laws addressed to a specific ecological context. NEPA's policy, values, and visions not only articulate the synergistic attributes of the natural world but also recognize the symbiotic relationship between humans, the economy, and the environment.

In addition, NEPA is unique because it not only integrates environmental goals but also cuts across a broad range of societal goals and concerns—economic, aesthetic, ethical, sociological, psychological, and ecological. Although there is a growing movement to revitalize NEPA, the law that has been described as America's environmental Magna Carta has paradoxically not become a highly visible centerpiece in environmental law and is virtually unknown to most Americans.

When NEPA is cited, it is discussed in terms of its environmental impact statement requirements. In Professor Caldwell's testimony regarding the Senate bill (S. 1075), he emphasized the practical implementation of NEPA's general goals.

> The Congress indeed has a responsibility to develop and could enunciate such a policy [for the environment]. But beyond this, I would urge that in the shaping of such policy, it have an action-forcing, operational

aspect. When we speak of policy, we ought to think of a statement which is so written that it is capable of implementation; that it is not merely a statement of things hoped for; not merely a statement of desirable goals or objectives; but that it is a statement which will compel or reinforce or assist all of these things in the executive agencies in particular, but going beyond this, in the nation as a whole, to take the kind of action which will protect and reinforce . . . [the] life support system of this country. . . .

A statement of policy by the Congress should at least consider measures to require the federal agencies, in submitting proposals, to contain within the proposals an evaluation of the effect of these proposals upon the state of the environment, that in the licensing procedures of the various agencies such as the Atomic Energy Commission or the Federal Power Commission or the Federal Aviation Agency there should also be, to the extent that there may not now exist fully or adequately, certain requirements with respect to environmental protection.[12]

Yet, while the EIS has certainly evolved into a very important tool for recognizing environmental consequences of federal actions, its overall effectiveness is weakened when NEPA's guiding ethical statements on environmental goals (sec. 101) are dismissed by government agencies and courts. In fact, the EIS requirement as stipulated by section 102 was intended simply to be an "action-forcing" mechanism to implement NEPA's important substantive goals addressed in section 101. In short, it is woefully myopic to view NEPA as a procedural law only. NEPA is not a regulatory statute. Rather, it is a statement about values and ethics that create institutions and rules for implementing environmental values. By revisiting NEPA's legislative history in chapter 3, we focus on locating the primary motives and intentions of NEPA's authors and major congressional supporters. This historical and contextual approach illustrates how the procedural tool—the EIS mechanism—was supposed to be linked to NEPA's broader policy goals.

Ethical foundations, of course, serve no purpose without sound and effective execution of policy. NEPA's environmental impact assessment does indeed force agencies to follow new procedures; although the connection between the assessment and a deeper understanding of ecological thinking is all but ignored by those who see the EIS as an end in itself. As explained by Caldwell in a 1998 book,

Impact assessment as a process and technique appeared during the latter half of the 20th century in response to consequences, unforseen and unwanted, of rapidly expanding technological innovation and economic development. Several forms of analysis and assessment emerged, including environmental, socioeconomic, technological, and comparative risk assessment and extended cost-benefit analysis. Of these, environmental impact assessment gained prominence, being [an] intergral [part] to the National Environmental Policy Act of 1969. The direct purpose of NEPA Section 102(2)(c) was to force agency attention to the substantive Section 101 provisions of the Act.[13]

NEPA's execution has faltered largely because of executive and judicial failure to implement, enforce, and interpret NEPA's broad policy objectives. Rather than recognizing the comprehensive core and long-term view embedded within NEPA, most U.S. presidents, agencies, and courts have applied a very narrow, crabbed interpretation in implementing NEPA. Most of them have incorporated and recognized only the EIS requirement and not the entire NEPA statement of environmental policy. The partial and incremental use of the law has weakened its eVectiveness and nearly obliterated the act's holistic purpose and vision.

An important factor in this misinterpretation has been the significant role the courts have played in narrowing NEPA's effectiveness. Judicial decisions—in addition to some federal agencies antagonistic to NEPA's vision—have seriously undermined the act's effectiveness. Like the interdependence of ecosystem components, policy formation and implementation consist of many interconnected factors that, woven together, determine NEPA's current place in U.S. politics. A full accounting of these factors and their interactions is the only accurate way to truly understand what NEPA signifies in contemporary environmental law and politics.

As the pressure of human activities on the environment increases, we must envision and adopt ecologically sustainable economies and public policies. If fully implemented according to its original intent, NEPA could represent a political device to guide Americans toward sustainable ecological paradigms. Indeed, NEPA expresses values that are widely held by many Americans. NEPA is a unique political achievement insofar as it creates an institutional foundation for preventive environmental planning to flourish.

Charting New Policy Terrain

The now-ubiquitous concept known as the "environment" began to take shape as a policy concept around 1963, the year Indiana University Professor Lynton K. Caldwell published his path-breaking and self-explanatory article "Environment: A New Focus for Public Policy?" Despite the criticism of Caldwell's early projections and environmental analysis, Rachel Carson, Stewart Udall, Barry Commoner, and others were also cautioning the American public and U.S. policy makers that the "environment" was more than the sum of all its parts and that public policy ought to address the holistic nature of ecosystems.[14] The importance of science, particularly ecosystems theory, to emerging environmental consciousness cannot be underestimated. The centerpiece of this recognition is the language of the National Environmental Policy Act of 1969, whose purposes, as stated in section 2, are profoundly and ecologically astute: "The purposes of this Act [see appendix A] are: To declare a national policy which will encourage productive and enjoyable harmony between man and his environment; to promote efforts which will prevent or eliminate damage to the environment and biosphere and stimulate the health and welfare of man; to enrich the understanding of the ecological systems and natural resources important to the Nation; and to establish a Council on Environmental Quality."[15]

NEPA, the Courts, and the Bureaucracy

As Lettie McSpadden Wenner and others have pointed out, environmental protection was rooted historically in English common law.[16] NEPA represented a 180-degree turn in the way the environment was treated by the courts. Signed into law in 1970 by President Nixon, NEPA catalyzed a shift from common law to statutory public law, as Congress followed NEPA by enacting an unprecedented number of environmental statutes throughout the 1970s.

Often when there is a broad statutory mandate, especially in "public-interest" laws, its implementation is often reduced to the lowest legal common denominator—the procedural requirement. As a result, the courts, hesitant to adjudicate on substantive grounds, focus on whether the implementing agency has met the procedural requirements. This reinforces agencies' attention to procedure over content. Thus, laws that were originally passed to achieve broad goals become bare-minimum procedural rules devoid of their original values and visions. For many federal agencies this is what NEPA has become—to the chagrin of ecologists but to the delight of bureaucratic bean counters who have an agency mission to fulfill and do not want any roadblocks stopping their "progress."

Nevertheless, quite clearly, NEPA continues to have a significant impact on the federal bureaucracy.[17] As Helen Ingram and Daniel Dreyfus asserted, NEPA has "intruded into the most remote recesses of the federal administrative machinery and influences the multitude of decisions being made by thousands of officials." Serge Taylor, author of *Making Bureaucracies Think*, points out that "three systematic failings of government decision processes . . . were addressed by NEPA: (1) advantage [had] not [been] taken of long planning periods to search for possible impacts and to explore design options, (2) important early choice points in agency decision processes were not visible or accessible to other agencies or the public, and (3) there were only weak norms of analysis underlying the creation, sharing, and criticism of empirical information."[18] NEPA addressed these administrative shortcomings by requiring disclosure of all draft and final impact statements, mandating public comment on proposed action by public agencies, and creating the CEQ to shepherd agency coordination and interpretation of the law.

Lynton Caldwell has identified four reasons that help explain the gap between the policy declared by NEPA and what actually occurs in government and the private economic sector: "The first is official marginalization of NEPA policy in deference to political parties; the second is judicial misinterpretation; the third is popular indifference to matters of principle when no compelling event arouses concern; and the fourth is the lag between conventional perceptions of the environment and the world dynamics of environmental change."[19] It is our hope that this book will improve public understanding of the law that reshaped federal administrative decision making.

Conclusion

The National Environmental Policy Act is one of the most significant federal environmental policies and has affected the U.S. political landscape for more than thirty years. NEPA was originally intended as a mechanism to hold federal agencies accountable for a misuse of the natural environment and, perhaps more important, to prevent environmental neglect in the first place by providing a broad policy to follow and a specific tool to ensure adherence to NEPA policy. Due to a number of factors, NEPA's impact domestically has evolved from a visionary policy declaration initially enforced by the lower federal courts to a manipulated and misunderstood statute that needs to be thoroughly revitalized by federal agencies and courts, and most important, fully enforced by the president who takes an oath to "faithfully execute the laws."

The time has come for scholars, policy makers, bureaucrats, environmental groups, and the public to fully and accurately understand NEPA's successes and failures. The key to understanding NEPA's applicability begins with a better public understanding of the law coupled with strong political leadership regarding environmental principles and priorities. If NEPA's intent is to be achieved, we must motivate the political forces to act in a fashion that resembles the nation's latent (and sometimes overt) preference in sound environmental policy. This requires a fundamental reassessment of societal priorities and political leaders who can revitalize NEPA's comprehensive policy for sustainable choices that seek to balance economics with ethics, equity, and ecology. We hope to further such an understanding in this book by addressing the act's larger theoretical, historical, and legal contexts.

The most critical assumptions and policy goals of NEPA are based on ecological science and values—insights undoubtedly present throughout recent history but all too often buried beneath the rubble, rubric, and demands of industrialism, individualism, and unfettered economic growth. The surfacing of ecological thinking in the late 1960s out of the often slow-moving toils of Congress was a legislative feat not noticed by most Americans and largely unappreciated and misunderstood by the majority of environmental organizations and scholars (see chap. 2). NEPA is a succinct, straightforward policy for the environment. Even though conventional wisdom may suggest that environmentalism is much more popular today than thirty years ago, it is paradoxically very doubtful that if NEPA were introduced today it would have much support in Congress. In fact, it is doubtful that a contemporary version of NEPA could be passed by today's Congress.[20]

Furthermore, and not surprisingly, there is disagreement among researchers about the locus and extent of NEPA's impact. Plater, Abrams, and Goldfarb correctly assert that, "NEPA. . . is a statute that provides a wild diversity of reactions. To some it is a paper tiger, of awesome but toothless aspect. To others it is a ringing statutory declaration of environmental protection and rational human governance, setting a precedent of international significance. To some it is an unproductive attempt to intrude on ongoing public-private enterprises. To others it is a legislative accident (whether fortunate or unfortunate) that was created and continues to evolve by happenstance. As usual, there is probably some truth in each of these perspectives."[21]

It is clear that NEPA attempted to institutionalize environmental values in decision making, and altered the bureaucratic decision processes with respect to who participates and with what leverage. Previous legislation, as well as much environmental legislation that followed NEPA, had treated environmental issues in a very isolated, problem-specific fashion. NEPA's intent and purpose was to lay out a national policy for the environment in the most comprehensive manner. While on special assignment for Senator Henry Jackson, who introduced NEPA legislation in the Senate, Caldwell wrote what Senator Jackson later introduced as Senate Bill 1075. The bill declared a wide range of environmental values for the nation and required an analysis of environmental effects in addition to economic considerations involved in any proposed "major federal action."[22] The idea that some economic benefits be forgone or balanced with social and environmental considerations in order to achieve or foster an environmental goal was a very radical shift in policy priorities and premises in the United States. Environmental quality was the intent of, but not necessarily the result of, NEPA. This book explains why this is the case.

NEPA's legal history has spawned hundreds of articles and books.[23] In addition to following NEPA's juridical evolution, numerous scholars have addressed NEPA's environmental impact statement requirement. It is beyond the scope of this book to synthesize all the literature about NEPA. It is this book's goal to document the larger congressional context of NEPA in order to understand the intended purpose of NEPA as a full accounting measure for the natural environment and to examine the failure of federal courts and executive agencies to implement this goal. We review the evolution of this unique statute and, in particular, attempt to provide a thorough accounting of NEPA's congressional, judicial, and executive implementation.

NEPA's Political and Social Origins

This chapter is retrospective, examining NEPA from two integrated perspectives: first, a brief historical sketch of natural resource and environmental politics in the United States prior to NEPA; second, NEPA's evolution from idea to law in the halls of Congress. The historical context explains NEPA's emergence in Congress, especially the comprehensive and visionary goals of NEPA's authors. This chapter reviews significant trends in both science and politics that led to the rise of environmental concerns and political activity. It also examines the original text of NEPA, its authors' fundamental assumptions, and the political climate leading up to and surrounding NEPA's passage. This task primarily involves investigating the historical underpinnings of contemporary ecological awareness in the United States, the congressional hearings and other testimony about NEPA, and criticism of NEPA.

So readers can better appreciate the history and implementation of NEPA, we first offer three general comments—or perhaps caveats—regarding the policy-formation process generally and the notion of administrative discretion specifically. First, it is common in the policy-formation process for legislation to be written in broad and ambiguous terms. As James Anderson has said, "Those who participate in the legislative process frequently are unable or unwilling to arrive at precise settlements of the conflicting interests on many issues. Only by leaving some matters somewhat nebulous and unsettled can agreement on legislation be reached."[1]

Second, the bargaining and compromise necessary for securing a majority for passage of legislation may produce laws that at least partially satisfy the conflicting needs of the participants in the legislative process but may not result in clearly defined, unambiguous legislative mandates. Several early versions of NEPA were modified to satisfy the various policy makers involved in NEPA's formation. As a result, some of NEPA's teeth were extracted or blunted.

Third, statutory ambiguity, the articulation of broad societal goals, or both also increase the discretionary power of the administrators and agencies charged with implementing regulations. Like all statutes, NEPA has its share of ambiguity. For example, NEPA's early definition of "major federal action" was up to each agency, although the Council on Environmental Quality is statutorily responsible for the act's executive oversight and has issued regulations defining NEPA's language. Furthermore, NEPA declares it federal policy to create "productive harmony between man and his environment." Lacking clarification of this concept, groups such as the National Manufacturers Association and the Sierra Club, and federal agencies such as the Department of Defense and the Fish and Wildlife Service will have drastically different views on what "productive harmony" means. Agency discretion and the varying interpretations of NEPA's language provide fertile ground for judicial intervention and clarification (see chap. 6). Hence, the variety of NEPA's interpretation and implementation could be anticipated in a policy-making process prone to ambiguity and an implementation process that allows administrative discretion. Indeed, both ambiguity and discretion played important roles in the development, passage, and implementation of NEPA.

The origins of NEPA include many influences. Its various ideological and political components were a function of a changing U.S. political climate and the evolution of environmental ethics. The nature of philosophical thinking that preceded NEPA's legislative process is interesting for policy analysis because it sheds light on the development and nature of environmental politics and policy today. "Environmentalism" has come to signify many things. Historically, the politics of environmentalism centered around specific issues, such as species loss or air quality. In NEPA's case, environmental groups were not a major factor in its legislative history. In fact, as Lynton Caldwell has stated, "NEPA was not a product of activist environmental groups or 'blue-ribbon' presidential commissions; its genesis occurred within the Congress, responding in a statesman-like manner to a perception of national interest."[2] However, a window of opportunity opened up for NEPA because of an emerging environmental movement that called attention to growing urban smog and assorted human-created ecological disasters.[3]

The authors of NEPA intended to break new ground. For the first time, federal legislation articulated a set of national values and goals rooted in an ecological understanding of the world. These principles of sustainable yield, energy efficiency, recycling, and environmental ethics were intended to inspire and enhance all future policies. NEPA was unique in that it legislated a holistic philosophy that challenged the status quo—the pursuit of economic growth and development regardless of the environmental effects. Although comprehensive environmental management is still a concern today in environmental administration and policy, NEPA represents one of the first federal attempts to view and implement environmental policy comprehensively. NEPA's articulated values for environmental policy affect the innermost machinery of government administration and influence myriad decisions made by thousands of federal and state officials.[4] At least four key aspects of NEPA significantly altered the policy-making process within federal agencies. First, the statute mandated the incorporation of a broad set of environmental goals. Second, the law and CEQ guidelines institutionalized a uniform "action-forcing" mechanism to ensure compliance with these ecological goals. Third, NEPA required that public participation be a part of the decision-making process. Fourth, the act established the CEQ. In short, for almost every federal agency, corporation, lawyer, and not-for-profit organization that works with the natural environment, political decision making was never the same again.

NEPA's Heritage: Public Participation and Discourse Leading to NEPA

The debate over NEPA took place within a political context beginning to be more predisposed to environmental awareness and preventive action. The ideas circulating in the late 1960s were preceded by those of earlier environmental scientists and writers.

The dominant attitudes and assumptions of the industrial era of the early 1900s were directly challenged by the writings of an early ecological critic,

Aldo Leopold. A forester by training, Leopold describes his relationship with the natural landscape in his classic book *A Sand County Almanac.* There he offers his oft-cited "land ethic": "A thing is right when it tends to preserve the integrity, stability, and beauty of the biotic community. It is wrong when it tends otherwise."[5] Leopold's influence, as an author, teacher, professional state forester, and founder of the Wilderness Society, contributed to a budding national concern about resource preservation, restoration ecology, and ecological thinking in policy making.

Beginning in the 1950s, the quality of the environment, particularly the water, land, and air proximate to human existence, was, according to historian Samuel Hays, "an integral part of the new search for a higher standard of living." Hays contended that the environment became an issue that resonated throughout the middle class of the 1950s and 1960s. As the booming postwar American middle class achieved a greater degree of financial and material wealth, pockets of the political culture adopted what Ronald Inglehart called "post-materialist" values paradigms. In extensive writings, Inglehart and his colleagues have shown an empirical relationship between the fulfillment of material needs and a greater concern for nonmaterial goods such as cleaner air, biodiversity, and other environmental public goods.[6]

In 1962 Rachel Carson's *Silent Spring* grabbed the attention of many Americans who were previously unaware of the harmful effects pesticides and other man-made chemicals have on the environment, both rural and urban. Carson not only described the chemical origins of environmental problems but also called on the public to embrace a more harmonious relationship with nature, rather than one that seeks to exploit and manipulate the environment for short-term economic gains (e.g., using DDT, paving over wetlands, and clear-cutting forests). Carson's work provided a stern challenge to her peers in the disengaged scientific community, which had previously shied away from normative political positions.

The list of academics that contributed to growing public concerns about environmental problems during this period is long. Those who made significant contributions included, but were not limited to, Barry Commoner, Paul and Anne Ehrlich, and Garrett Hardin. Commoner, a socialist and biologist who first focused his efforts on the problems of nuclear technologies, became especially well known when his book *The Closing Circle* was published in 1971. Paul and Anne Ehrlich, both population biologists at Stanford University, brought population issues to the public's attention. In 1968 Paul Ehrlich wrote *The Population Bomb,* which illustrates many of the common pool resource issues Garrett Hardin wrote about in his famous essay "The Tragedy of the Commons."[7]

Once the salience of nature and the planet's health as a political issue had been raised, several natural crises further shifted attention to pollution and conservation issues. In January and February, 1969, two oil spills five and a half miles off the coast of Santa Barbara, California, coated thirty miles of beaches and killed thousands of seabirds, fish, and other animals. John Whitaker, an adviser on environmental issues to President Nixon, believed the oil spill "was comparable to tossing a match into a gasoline tank: it exploded into the environmental revolution, and the press fanned the flames to keep the issue burning brightly."[8] Conservation groups, as well as public interest in recreation, were also on the rise. Many new groups, such as the World Wildlife Fund (1961), Environmental Defense Fund (1967), and Natural Resources Defense Council (1969) were formed during this time. Existing groups such as the Sierra Club and the National Audubon Society saw their membership triple.[9]

The Need for NEPA and a Comprehensive Environmental Policy

Although we can trace contemporary major federal environmental policies back to the 1955 Clean Air Act (CAA), earlier laws certainly dealt with the environment. Well before passage of the CAA, Congress in the late 1940s enacted some of the first federal protective measures for the environment and public health. Two of the post–World War II laws were the Insecticide, Fungicide, and Rodenticide Act of 1947 and the Water Pollution Control Act of 1948. Other than CAA in 1955, the 1950s did not present many significant initiatives in environmental law. The 1960s witnessed several innovations in environmental policy, including the creation of a federal wilderness system and the expansion of federal concern over many issues from pollution control to solid waste disposal problems.[10] Some of these measures include:

Clean Water Act of 1960
Partial Nuclear Test Ban Treaty of 1963
Wilderness Act of 1964
Water Quality Act of 1965
Solid Waste Disposal Act of 1965

Yet these and other legislative acts passed at that time were focused on specific issues. Until the passage of NEPA, attempts to deal with environmental issues were routinely isolated, ad hoc, and incremental. Beginning in the early 1960s, many federal environmental policies began dealing with water resources planning, air and water pollution control, and recreation, but this problem-to-problem approach neglected the cleavages, lack of boundaries, and interdependency between these issues. The evolution of federal institutions lacked a clear doctrine and locus of political responsibility for the whole natural environment. As a result, environmental quality was the business of a scattered few in public office. Prior to NEPA, political institutions at all levels of government affected the environment; however, public policies had yet to view "environments as entities different from the sum total of their parts."[11] In other words, each federal agency directed its own agendas and policies regarding the environment. In most cases, this meant in the final analysis that ecological values were given little weight. Consequently, the holistic nature of ecosystems and of environmental problems was often disregarded by policy makers. Each federal agency claimed a narrowly defined mission of its own that dealt with the environment as an isolated issue. This administrative problem stemmed from segmented public policy. Different states had conflicting policies, which were themselves fragmented, and there was very little overall federal legislation. Furthermore, one set of federal laws might govern a source of pollution when it originated on land, another when it moved into the air, still another when it entered a body of water. Today, these problems are referred to as "multimedia management problems."

As Caldwell first noted in "Environment: A New Focus for Public Policy?" "Segmental thinking [and] segmental decision making [have] again and again produced some very impractical results." Furthermore, he asserted elsewhere, "It can be demonstrated that many of the worst environmental errors have been consequences of . . . [a] failure to perceive specific environmental situations in comprehensive ecological terms." When "the environment" is perceived, for example, merely as an antipollution issue, the focus and energy directed at grappling with pollution may overlook other ecological matters. Policymakers have historically taken "the [overall] environment for granted [and] have dealt with its various elements without regard to their interrelated totality."[12] Consequently, governments often try to put out little fires (isolated pollution problems, for example) at the expense of larger ones (the interrelated environmental problems that are part of larger ecological systems). Critics of piecemeal administrative treatment of the environment argued that because ecosystems are interconnected and comprehensive, public policies need to address the environment in a comprehensive manner. In this sense, NEPA and CEQ's implementing language offer an ecological or ecosystem approach to both the organization of federal planning and the impact of federal actions and decisions.

Although ecosystems are interrelated and sound environmental policies require a more unified approach, this unified approach is often quite difficult to accomplish because there are entrenched institutional (internal) and societal (external) interests that greatly benefit from a fragmented approach to environmental policy. In addition, the concept of government planning in the United States arouses a maelstrom of emotions and conflicts among property owners, opponents of globalization, and manufacturers of all the energy-intensive products we consume. Yet without a relatively cohesive environmental plan in the executive branch, there are many contradictory agendas and decisions, because each agency caters to different and often competing client interests. The agrochemical industry, for example, would understandably prefer that a decision on the approval of a new pesticide be made by the Department of Agriculture, a department geared toward improving the well-being of its primary client, the agriculture industry. As numerous scholars have pointed out, powerful interest groups benefit from fragmented environmental decision making.[13]

The Beginning of NEPA

In 1963 Caldwell proposed a radically new concept of "environmental administration" as a vehicle for conceptualizing the total environment in public policies. This, however, does not mean endless analysis of every single detail in all the environmental factors involved in public planning and development processes. As Caldwell noted, "There is a common-sense balance between the too-often uninformed, expedient, piecemeal method now generally pursued and a perfectionist effort to take into account absolutely everything relevant to a contemplated environmental change." To facilitate a uniform and more balanced approach within federal environmental administration, Caldwell articulated the need for a "totalizing concept of environmental development that [would] provide a common denominator among differing values and interests."[14] He articulated a national need for a unifying set of environmental principles and the tools to achieve them. A reconciliation of economic and environmental values was a primary goal of NEPA. Its authors believed in balancing our multiple interests over the long term within a framework that understands environmental quality to be a fundamental goal.

Effective environmental policy requires the intersection of policy values with policy instruments or tools. Caldwell, one of the first scholars to argue this, first developed these thoughts in a 1964 unpublished paper entitled "Making Environmental Concepts Operational." Here, he developed a ten point rational that clearly mirrors NEPA's language.

1. Man's manipulation of the physical aspects of his environment is proceeding at an accelerating rate.

2. Pressure on environmentalists generated by increasing populations, rising demands upon national resources, and rapidly expanding technologies indicate the probability of radical and far-reaching environmental changes in the years ahead.

3. Environmental and ecological science have not grown at a pace commensurate either with human demands upon the environment or with the technological means of pursuing these demands.

4. The individuals and organizations that plan and execute policies affecting the environment cannot, in the absence of informed assistance, be expected to appreciate ecological relationships or to understand the implication of environmental change.

5. On the basis of statistical probability and historical experience, a large number of ecological errors, ranging from the inconvenient to the catastrophic, can be predicted in rough proportion to the increasing tempo of environmental change.

6. Although some of these errors will be unavoidable, others need not occur if action is guided by existing knowledge. However, in the absence of far more widespread and practical methods of environmental decision making than we have today, many of these mistakes *will* occur *even* when the knowledge to avoid them is actually available.

7. Human societies need not—indeed cannot—afford to incur an unnecessarily high cost in ecological errors, some of which could easily be disastrous for all mankind.

8. If the number and severity of these errors are to be reduced, rapid, far-reaching systematic improvement of ecological and environmental decision making is necessary.

9. The normal processes of education alone are too slow and too abstract to bring the perceptions, values, and understanding of people as rapidly as need be into consistency with valid scientific knowledge of environmental and ecological relationships.

10. Some instrumental means are therefore needed to improve the quality of decision making on environmental and ecological matters, and which can be successfully applied under conditions wherein ecological sophistication is minimal.[15]

NEPA was created in response to organizational fragmentation and lack of national environmental priorities. NEPA was to shape national policy around a core set of guidelines rooted in ecological values and an awareness of other than economic needs. It was the intention of NEPA's authors that a coordinated and comprehensive analysis of ecological and social impacts of federal decision making replace the ad hoc, fragmented status quo in policy formulation. This analysis is the impact statement process. In his influential essay "A National Policy for the Environment," Caldwell explained his thinking to members of Congress:

Our present governmental organization has not been designed to deal with environmental policy in any basic or coherent manner. The extent to which governmental reorganization may be necessary cannot be determined absolutely in advance of experience. But it does seem probable that some new facility will be needed to provide a point at which environmental policy issues cutting across jurisdictional lines of existing agencies can be identified and analyzed, and at which the complex problems involved in man's relationships with his environment can be reduced to questions and issues capable of being studied, debated, and acted upon by the President, the Congress, and the American people.

To effectively reconcile a wide range of political and economic interests, a policy model for the environment must be compatible and consistent with many other needs to which the nation must respond. But it must also define the intent of the American people toward the management of their environment in terms that the Congress, the President, the administrative agencies, and the electorate can consider and act upon. A national policy for the environment must be [a] principle which can be applied in action. The goals of effective environmental policy cannot be counsels of perfection; what the nation requires are guidelines to assist the government, private enterprise, and the individual citizen to plan together and to work together toward meeting the challenge of a better environment.[16]

The idea of the EIS requirement, written into law as section 102 of NEPA, attempted to strike a balance among interests. However, Caldwell had warned that the EIS alone might "facilitate, but would not lessen, the political task of reconciling a great diversity of interests and values."[17]

Ian McHarg, a landscape architect and urban planner, was also influential in arguing for more systematic ecological planning. McHarg's book, *Design with Nature*, published in 1969, called for planning that was more consistent with ecological factors. McHarg's multidisciplinary approach to evaluating ecological impacts was directly adapted into NEPA statutory language that addressed holistic decision making. McHarg has since served as an informal adviser to several CEQ members.

Crisis Prerequisites for Policy Formation

While administrative policy, for the most part, is constructed in an incremental fashion, by contrast the political system takes large leaps in time of emergency or crisis.[18] In representative democracies, a crisis may be necessary to instigate significant actions or major changes in public policy. This often explains the formation of environmental policy in the United

States.[19] In a noncrisis political climate, of course, public policy usually reverts to being developed and redeveloped incrementally. The trade-offs, bargaining, and compromising character of the policy-making process during normal times can be greatly streamlined during times of crisis. A notable example in U.S. history is the Great Depression. When Franklin D. Roosevelt was elected president by a landslide in 1932, the country had been in a serious economic depression for almost three years. During Franklin Roosevelt's first hundred days in office, the policy process was streamlined by a sense of urgency and the force of Roosevelt's personality and persuasion, so record amounts of new legislation were introduced and passed. A crisis might happen overnight or, as in the case of the Great Depression, build over a long period but eventually the perception is created that action must be taken immediately.

There is every reason to believe that the policy-making system will respond to environmental problems that are perceived to be an emergency—those requiring immediate action. For example, the Three Mile Island nuclear reactor accident resulted in relatively swift change in the policies of the Nuclear Regulatory Commission. In addition, much of the major environmental legislation passed in the early 1970s in the United States was a direct response to a profound sense of urgency concerning environmental quality.

Although the policy-formation process can and does respond to crises or emergencies, many policies are weakened during the implementation stage. For example, the discovery of a toxic dump at "Love Canal" in Buffalo, New York, and related health effects in Niagara Falls surely added impetus to the passage of the Comprehensive Environmental Response, Compensation, and Liability Act, otherwise known as the Superfund, in 1980. Nevertheless, the Superfund in its implementation currently finds itself buried in stagnation and policy drift while the various players battle over the scope and power of the act.

Due to a variety of factors, environmental policy issues are rarely cast, and are usually difficult to cast, in crisis terms. Many environmental problems, such as climate change, the discovery of polluted groundwater, the depletion of fossil fuel resources, and global warming progress slowly, sometimes without noticeable or dramatic change from one month or one year to the next. This slow progression is ideally suited to incremental decision making and also does not disrupt or challenge the short-term goals of elected policy makers or the ideological pressure from the business community toward growth and development. In sum, environmental problems often lead to short-term and partial solutions.

In an introductory report regarding early NEPA bills and discussion, Senator Henry Jackson summed up NEPA's purpose of changing incremental environmental policy: "Throughout much of our history, the goal of managing the environment for the benefit of all citizens has often been overshadowed and obscured by the pursuit of narrower and more immediate economic goals. . . . This report proposes that the American people, the Congress, and the Administration break the shackles of incremental policy making in the management of the environment."[20]

Motivated by a sense of crisis and urgency, the public clearly led the way in formulating dissent over the status quo in environmental administration and policy. As Caldwell stated in a 1989 article, "In comprehending the importance of environmental degradation, the public was the path breaker—generally ahead of Congress, and far ahead of the White House."[21] The conditions were set for an overwhelming congressional and public push for a national policy for the environment. This political climate produced, among other things, NEPA.

NEPA's Legislative History

Because NEPA is constantly being interpreted in the courts, and is a day-to-day activity for many environmental planners, it is important to take a close look at the political context of its creation and its drafters' intentions. The intentions of a statute's authors are important because they may play a role in subsequent judicial and administrative interpretations of the respective policy. Frequently, the courts will look to a law's legislative history as a basis for establishing congressional intent. Given the U.S. Supreme Court's curbed interpretations of NEPA, a thorough investigation of NEPA's legislative history is not only prudent but also long overdue.

The authors of NEPA intended more from their work than the watered-down, expensive, procedural paper chase that characterizes NEPA's implementation in federal agencies today. While some environmental law professors contend that "there really wasn't any . . . intention of the legislature,"[22] we fundamentally disagree. In essence, Congress intended that environmental, social, and other impacts not only be researched and published in the planning process but, perhaps more important, also be evaluated with respect to NEPA's overall conservation ethic and its requirement that measures be put in place to mitigate the environmentally damaging effects of federal actions. NEPA required agencies to fully investigate their decisions and to include the public in their planning. During floor deliberations on the nearly complete NEPA, Senator Jackson maintained that NEPA was important because it dealt "with environmental problems on a preventive and an anticipatory basis," instead of with a crisis mentality that focuses on reclaiming "our resources from past abuses."[23]

Interestingly, NEPA was not the first congressional attempt to address environmental policy in a systematic way. On August 20, 1959, Senator James Murray (D-Mont.), as chair of the Senate Committee on Interior and Insular Affairs, introduced Senate Bill 2549, a national conservation policy proposal that argued for stronger public responsibility for protecting and managing natural resources. Although the bill did not use the term "environment" as its linguistic focus, S. 2549 did contain a statement of national policy on "conservation, development, and utilization of natural resources."[24] The operational aspect of the bill was the creation of a council of resources and conservation as advisers to the president. In many ways, this foreshadowed the Council of Environmental Quality. In January, 1960, hearings were held on the Murray Bill (which had thirty cosponsors), but legislation failed to materialize largely due to opposition by the Eisenhower administration and by powerful federal agencies and business interest groups. Although Senator Murray did not run for reelection in 1960, his bill was reintroduced by Senator Clair Engle (D-Calif.), and a similar bill was introduced by Senator Gale McGee (D-Mont.) in 1961. The Kennedy administration was interested in environmental policy and the Murray Bill had been endorsed in the 1960 Democratic platform.

However, Kennedy moved indecisively toward establishing a national policy for the environment. Both the Kennedy administration and federal agencies opposed the Murray and McGee bills, and neither bill came out of the Senate Interior Committee. Senators McGee and George McGovern (D-S.Dak.) introduced similar bills in 1963 and 1965, respectively, again without success. Because the worsening environmental conditions continued to be defined as isolated pollution or natural resource issues, the solutions were seen as technological and economic. Despite ecology's standing as a science today, ecological studies were sparse and regarded as "second-class" science even as late as the early 1960s. NEPA is important because the policy goals and impact statement procedures reflect a desire to incorporate systems theory and, specifically, ecology into federal planning.

Natural resource policy issues became a higher priority during the Johnson administration. While the executive branch pursued its conservation priorities, Congress pressured it, especially the Department of Interior, to become more focused on environmental values and considerations.[25] But as with U.S. environmental policy throughout the early twentieth century, President Lyndon Johnson approached the protection of the natural environment predominantly from a resource conservation perspective. In the much-heralded 1965 White House Conference on Natural Beauty, Johnson noted the value of aesthetic beauty, and the Highway Beautification Act grew, in part, out of that conference. That same year, Johnson proclaimed in his State of the Union address a "creed" to protect our natural history and resources. Johnson also commissioned a president's Science Advisory Committee, which issued a report in November, 1965, *Restoring the Quality of Our Environment: Report of the Environmental Pollution Panel.* However, the spirit and momentum initiated by these conferences and reports dissipated as President Johnson became increasingly involved with the Vietnam War and the strong negative reactions to the war in the United States.

The first time the term "ecology" appeared in a legislative proposal was in Senator Gaylord Nelson's Ecological Research and Surveys Bill (S. 2282) of 1965. The bill did not make it out of committee, but its proposal for a council of environmental advisers was later partially incorporated into NEPA as Title II. Nelson's bill would have set up a federal system for collecting data pertaining to the natural environment. Oversight responsibilities were to be placed under the jurisdiction of the Interior Department. Although Nelson's bill was never enacted, it was a critical shift in legislative responses toward natural resources policy. Prior to Nelson's efforts, the few bills that did address the natural world were focused on individual resources such as timber, coal, and water or on the management of certain federal land by a specific agency rather than on an interconnected environmental whole.[26]

The Nelson bill shifted the focus of public policy to a more comprehensive notion of the "environment." The value of this level of analysis is based on the assumption that by looking at all the informational inputs into the ecological system, environmental policies will be more effective. When designing NEPA, Caldwell took this concept of information gathering a step further and argued that information reflecting environmental conditions should be directly incorporated into the system of agency decision making. NEPA's environmental impact statement requirement is an attempt to institutionalize and internalize the analysis of environmental effects and information into the federal bureaucratic decision making.

By the end of 1967, it seemed certain that some form of national legislation would be enacted to address growing dissatisfaction with environmental management. Indeed, by the late 1960s, 120 members of Congress had bills dealing with environmental issues referred to nineteen separate committees of the House and Senate. Congressional observers felt this constituted a jurisdictional nightmare for formation of a comprehensive national environmental policy both within Congress (there was initially little coordination among the competing bills) and, should any of them become law, within the numerous agencies and departments designated in the bills.[27] Because each federal agency viewed environmental assets and policy differently, the challenge for legislators in the late 1960s was to formulate comprehensive approaches for managing the environment.

The legislative movement for a broad national governmental policy gained momentum when the Subcommittee on Science, Research, and Development of the House Committee on Science and Astronautics published a report in 1968 entitled *Managing the Environment.*[28] At about the same time, several executive branch studies on environmental matters were commissioned and new proposals for administrative reorganization were introduced in both the executive and legislative branches.

The 1968 House-Senate Joint Environmental Colloquium

The most significant springboard for coordinating some type of national environmental policy was the House-Senate Joint Colloquium to Discuss the National Policy for the Environment on July 17, 1968. This seminal meeting between the Senate's Committee on Interior and Insular Affairs and the House of Representative's Committee on Science and Astronautics was convened at the capitol and cochaired by Senator Jackson, chair of the Senate committee, and Congressman George Miller (D-Calif.), chair of the House committee. This meeting, not called to address specific legislative proposals, was an "informal study session" that addressed environmental management, committee jurisdictions, the need for sounder environmental information, and "directions environmental policy should take."[29] Representatives from the 90th Congress, academia, and environmental groups were invited to participate in this event. Of central concern for the conference participants was the special report issued by the Senate's Committee on Interior and Insular Affairs entitled *A National Policy for the Environment* written by Lynton K. Caldwell with assistance from William Van Ness and Senator Jackson. This comprehensive essay proposed goals, visions, and agendas for a relatively unified federal environmental policy. Major concepts of this influential report were later incorporated into the first section of NEPA.

Laurence S. Rockefeller, who had chaired President Johnson's 1965 White House Conference on Natural Beauty, opened the colloquium's panel discussion. Rockefeller articulated the need for some institutional changes. "Our federal government structure is still designed for the problems of an earlier day. The basic allocation of responsibilities among departments reflects a nation which was predominantly rural, which had to dispose of its vast public lands and tame its rivers and forests. It is not designed for the complex, highly urban society in which we are now living, or the changed circumstances in our rural areas."[30] The need for a uniform, empowering set of environmental goals and guidelines for federal agencies was a primary concern at the colloquium. According to Rockefeller, this needed to be addressed because "we have not set down in clear terms what our goals are for the long-term future. Certainly no aspect of national life is more important to the health and welfare of our children and grandchildren" than quality environmental management and policies.[31]

Clearly the levers for changing environmental policy were in the hands of Congress. This colloquium spelled out a need for new legislation, and proposed ethical and administrative ideas for such legislation. Strengthening congressional overview was mentioned by several in Johnson's cabinet. Secretary of Interior Stewart L. Udall stressed this unequivocally: "I think Congress ought to be much less bashful about spending more money on strengthening its staff so it can provide the kind of oversight that is needed." Secretary of Health, Education, and Welfare Wilbur J. Cohen recommended "that Congress examine its own organization in order to improve its ability to deal in a comprehensive and coordinated manner with the total problem of environmental quality."[32]

The value of cost-benefit economic analysis as a vehicle for evaluating the economic and environmental impacts of policy decisions became a key debate at the colloquium. This planning tool, developed within neo-classical microeconomics assumptions, asserted that human beings can accurately and rationally collect, evaluate, analyze, quantify, and rank-order social and economic information in a comprehensive and objective fashion. However, in speaking of the need for greater consideration of environmental conditions in planning and development decisions, Rockefeller explained the inherent pitfall of cost-benefit analysis when used in environmental policy making: because "no one can tell us the cost of various alternatives in long-term environmental values. . . . [The] cost-benefit ratio does not adequately reflect environmental factors."[33] In fact, trying to figure out how to quantify environmental assets in cost-benefit analysis continues to be a major point of contention today.[34]

During the colloquium, Secretary Cohen spoke of the need for an "enlightened self-interest" in which industry and commerce recognize the long-term benefits environmental controls bring to industry and the general public.[35] In his report, Caldwell argued that all companies should recognize that "scientific knowledge and rising levels of amenity standards have added to public expectation that protection against environmental change will be built into the products and production costs of manufacturers."[36] Interior Secretary Udall seriously challenged the dominant paradigm of human mastery over nature. Udall asserted, "We must begin to work with, not against, the laws of the planet on which we live, rejecting once and for all the false notion that man can impose his will on nature." Secretary Udall also noted the importance of enhancing broad environmental policy goals and values "through new laws and new policies that reject the old ways."[37]

Following the colloquium, the Legislative Reference Service issued an influential congressional white paper summarizing and expanding on the arguments and concepts surrounding the colloquium. The urgency for recognizing "new" environmental values, aesthetics, and ethics was pointedly clear in the document. The environmental impact statement was needed, it was argued, to help implement these values in federal agency decision making.

Many of the institutional and environmental concerns and strategies of NEPA (especially the EIS provisions) were clearly embedded within the *Congressional White Paper.*

> Alteration and use of the environment must be planned and controlled rather than left to arbitrary decision. Alternatives must be actively generated and widely discussed. Technological development, introduction of new factors affecting the environment, and modifications of the landscape must be planned to maintain the diversity of plants and animals. Furthermore, such activities should proceed only after an ecological analysis and projection of probable effects. Irreversible or difficult reversible changes should be accepted only after the most thorough study.[38]

The breadth and importance of NEPA's stated language mandating comprehensive environmental planning by the federal government is exemplified in the statute's overall legislative history and in the following discussion of its congressional enactment.

CHAPTER 3

NEPA's Legislative History and Implications

NEPA's legislative genesis is primarily the work of Senator Henry Jackson, who first introduced it in Senate Bill 1075. Although numerous environmental bills were being circulated in the late 1960s, Jackson's bill became, after subsequent debate and revisions, the foundation upon which NEPA was built. Senator Jackson, as chair of the Senate Committee on Interior and Insular Affairs, and Congressman John Dingell (D-Mich.), chair of the House's Merchant Marine and Fisheries Committee, led NEPA through Congress. Both Jackson and Dingell recognized that the federal government lacked a cohesive and consistent policy toward the environment.

Political scientist Geoffrey Wandesforde-Smith has argued that there were two influential aspects in the pre-NEPA political climate. First, Wandesforde-Smith contended that the loosely connected, compartmentalized nature of pre-NEPA environmental management was solely oriented toward economic and agency growth. Every federal agency pursued its respective missions and objectives—with mitigating environmental consequences near the bottom of their priorities. Wandesforde-Smith also maintained that at the time of NEPA's passage, the perception had grown that federal government had an ethical responsibility as the agent of the people to manage the environment as steward or protective custodian for posterity. This required the abandonment of government's role as umpire among conflicting and competing resource interests and the adoption of the total environment as a focus for public policy.[1] In fact, the law's language in section 101 and the congressional reports are based on a positive or proactive role for government and on the importance of stewardship.

Drafting NEPA: The Senate

On February 18, 1969, S. 1075, the backbone of NEPA was introduced by Senator Jackson. Jackson regarded S. 1075 as a "working paper" for a national policy on environmental management.[2] As initially submitted, the bill was fairly limited. The central concern of S. 1075 was information gathering and oversight by an environmental council in the executive office. Jackson's bill included a preamble and two titles. The preamble, which contained the bill's goals, was not a comprehensive statement for a national environmental policy but did foreshadow some of the goals articulated in the final version of NEPA—especially NEPA's declaration of a national environmental policy. Title I of the original S. 1075 directed the secretary of the interior to conduct research on the state of the environment. Title II established an executive council on environmental quality, required an annual report, and granted the council a broad information-gathering function. This was the beginning of NEPA in the Senate. Similar initiatives were under way in the House, most important, Congressman Dingell's House Resolution 6750, which eventually emerged as the critical NEPA component from the House. In light of NEPA's subsequent history, it is important to note that there was no EIS provision in either of the original versions.

Structurally, NEPA was modeled in two ways after the Employment Act of 1946. First, the Employment Act set forth an economic agenda that created a national policy for maintaining a strong economy and made economic growth a major national goal that was to be a focus throughout federal government. Similarly, NEPA created a national policy for the environment that was supposed to permeate the federal government. Second, the Employment Act established a council of economic advisers to assist the president in creating and maintaining a healthy and prosperous economy. NEPA created the Council for Environmental Quality. In effect, NEPA's operative directions for environmental quality mirror the priority the Employment Act of 1946 gave to economic quality of life.[3]

On April 16, 1969, Senator Jackson and the Senate Committee on Interior and Insular Affairs conducted hearings on the original S. 1075. In the congressional hearings, witnesses testified from the executive branch, academia, business, and interest groups. The legislative record indicates that there was a general consensus, particularly from within the executive branch, for environmental oversight and advice.

In his subsequent report to the Senate Committee on Interior and Insular Affairs, Caldwell articulated the need for including much more information on environmental effects within the policy decision-making process. The need for more knowledge was well known; the challenge was to establish "a system to insure that existing knowledge and new findings will be organized in a manner suitable for review."[4] A comprehensive program for environmental administration necessarily involved incorporating the research, values, and opinions of a variety of academic disciplines and political agencies.

Caldwell's two "essential structural innovations" needed in a national environmental policy, the CEQ and the EIS, were subsequently incorporated into NEPA and, respectively, defined by Congress as "(a) a high-level reviewing and reporting agency and (b) an information-gathering and -organizing system." Jackson's original S. 1075 did not include any EIS provision. This idea of an "action-forcing mechanism" was introduced by Caldwell, who subsequently impressed upon Senator Jackson the importance of the impact statement documents. The systematic production and application of ecological knowledge could now take place within the EIS process. The institution for organizing and collecting new environmental information as well as overseeing NEPA's implementation was the Council on Environmental Quality. As Caldwell explained, this council was conceived as a "bridge between the functions of environmental surveillance, research, and analysis, on the one hand, and the policy-making functions of the President and the Congress on the other."[5]

Although representatives from various executive departments and agencies presented conflicting positions regarding the creation and structure of a new council during testimony and in written communications to the Senate committee, in general the Nixon administration had two major objections to S. 1075. First, while it agreed that environmental research should be institutionalized within the executive branch, it disagreed with Title I, which would grant the secretary of the Department of Interior a wide range of what it argued were potentially unconstitutional powers (based on the separation of powers).[6] Second, it reiterated President Nixon's belief that an executive-created council, such as Nixon had proposed to create by executive order within the White House, offered more flexibility than a council established by Congress.[7] So the Nixon administration opposed the creation of any new executive office by congressional act. Senator Jackson responded that a permanent congressionally mandated council would be better because it would be less apt to show departmental bias and better able to tackle long-term environmental problems. There was, however, a widespread legislative and executive agreement that environmental responsibility should be simplified and centralized.[8]

A number of suggestions were made during committee deliberations over S. 1075 concerning the authority any new agency would have. Anthony Wayne Smith, former president and general counsel of the National Parks Association, suggested that the council have the power to veto, at least temporarily, any projects deemed to be too environmentally harmful. He stated that this "stop-order authority" was extremely important. According to Smith, other executive councils, such as former President Johnson's Council on Recreation and Natural Beauty and the Water Resources Council, had been largely ineffective in protecting the environment because they had little authority to act against proposed projects or policies deemed harmful. Moreover, Smith testified that "we have had coordinating agencies which served merely to expedite the environmentally destructive activities of the existing agencies, to move them ahead ever more rapidly, to eliminate conflict among them, and in the end to make destruction more efficient."[9] The new council's stop-order power was considered by the committee's staff and discussed by the staff and Jackson. But the stop-order provision was not passed by the full committee because a majority did not want to authorize summary power for appointed officials.

S. 1075 was amended by the committee in a variety of important ways. First, Jackson introduced a provision on May 29, 1969, to establish citizens' "fundamental and inalienable right to a healthful environment and . . . responsibility to contribute to the preservation and enhancement of the environment."[10] Therefore, section 101(a) was made into a general philosophical statement of a national environmental policy. Second, Jackson and others, including Caldwell, believed that a universal environmental policy would serve as a benchmark against which federal actions could be judged. Finally, Jackson's amendments also included Caldwell's "action-forcing mechanism," codified as section 102 in NEPA. In his written report to the Senate Interior and Insular Affairs Committee, Caldwell argued that NEPA's general goals would have no effect unless the bill had some sort of "action-forcing mechanism" to ensure agencies' compliance with NEPA goals. Furthermore, Caldwell's written report mirrored Senator Jackson's bill in providing a broad set of environmental goals. He insisted that support for a national policy be enforced: "We ought to think of a statement which is so written that it is capable of implementation: that it is not merely a statement of things hoped for; not merely a statement of desirable goals or objectives; but that it is a statement which will compel or reinforce or assist all of these things, the executive agencies in particular, but going beyond this, the Nation as a whole, to take the kind of action which will protect and reinforce what I have called the life support system of this country."[11]

Besides forcing decisions and action to incorporate environmental factors, section 103 of Senate bill 1075 required all federal agencies to examine their regulations, statutes, and policies to ensure "conformity with the intent, purposes, and procedures set forth in this Act."[12] This measure was intended to override agency and administrative indifference to the environment by installing institutional requirements for including environmental values, effects, and alternatives in federal decision making. As Nicholas Yost contended, "It is clear that the 'action-forcing' procedures include those of Section 102—not only those the Committee termed the 'operating procedures' of Section 102(2), but also the provisions of Section 102(1) that link Section 102 to Section 101 and direct that all laws and regulations be interpreted and administered in light of section 101." As Richard N. L. Andrews argued, Caldwell's recommendation was a "radical and unprecedented innovation." The link between procedure and substance is of utmost importance: Caldwell called the connection between mandatory procedures and substantive criteria, the "genius" of NEPA.[13]

Caldwell envisioned the action-forcing requirement to be a mechanism that would force federal agencies to comply with the bill's goals—especially the consideration and evaluation of proposed projects' environmental ramifications. He argued that an EIS process should also affect the licensing procedures of independent regulatory agencies. Caldwell also urged giving the Bureau of the Budget an oversight role that would grant it the power to evaluate the environmental impact of proposed public works projects.

Senator Jackson proposed making the Bureau of the Budget use environmental information in its decision-making models. He believed this would prompt other federal agencies to adopt internal environmental considerations within their respective decision-making procedures. This hopeful, and perhaps naive, optimism was challenged by Senator Edmund S. Muskie (D-Maine) and by Caldwell; they persuaded Jackson that there needed to be an explicit and universal policy enforcement mechanism. With the creation of an executive environmental council, the Department of the Interior was deleted from Title I as an information-gathering source.

Section 102 of Title I was highly influenced by Caldwell's argument for an action-forcing mechanism (the EIS) to ensure compliance with the statute's general aims and goals. Section 102(b) was strengthened through the addition of Caldwell's EIS recommendation. The EIS language was subsequently drafted as a bill by Jackson staff members, William Van Ness and Daniel Dreyfus, assisted by Caldwell. The impact statement requirements were viewed by Dreyfus as the teeth to force agencies to "do something which they couldn't escape doing, and make them pay if they didn't." The EIS requirements were intended to pinpoint responsibility for investigating environmental findings on a specific individual or group of officials, thereby increasing accountability. NEPA's founders hoped that by detailing environmental findings and impacts of a proposed action, as well as requiring an investigation into all the options and their respective impacts, agency decision makers would give greater credence to the environmental impact of their projects. As Caldwell stated in his 1969 report to the Senate, "Fewer environmentally controversial decisions would be made because ecologically injurious projects would be denied serious consideration in their early stages."[14] This would be entirely true only if the values and goals NEPA set forth for the nation were always adhered to and executed by presidents and enforced in the courts. However, Caldwell's comments are illustrative of the theory behind the act. For the first time in history, the federal government could create a template for comprehensive environmental responsibility and accountability. Federal agency decisions could now be compared for consistency with NEPA's declared principles for environmental quality.

Nevertheless, amendments to section 103 addressed federal agencies' fears of the statute's jurisdictional aspects. The bill's sponsors did not want to antagonize the existing leadership of federal agencies. Hence, the Senate Committee on Interior and Insular Affair's report states that "the policies and goals set forth in this Act are amendatory and supplementary to, but shall not be considered to repeal, the existing mandates and authorizations of Federal agencies."[15] On June 18, 1969, the committee unanimously approved the amended version of S. 1075 and issued its report to the full Senate. On July 10, 1969, S. 1075 passed the Senate by a voice vote.[16] The tactical ability of Senator Jackson and William Van Ness ensured that S. 1075 was voted on during the "morning hour"—a period reserved for routine matters. Jackson's bill was passed without debate and with no further amendments. Meanwhile, the House was still debating similar legislation offered by Congressman John Dingell.

Drafting NEPA: Action in the U.S. House of Representatives

Action in the U.S. House of Representatives on a NEPA bill originated in the 91st Congress with H.R. 6750, submitted by Congressman John Dingell. H.R. 6750 was written as an amendment to the Fish and Wildlife Coordination Act, which was under the jurisdiction of Dingell's Subcommittee on Fisheries and Wildlife Conservation of the Committee on Merchant Marine and Fisheries. H.R. 6750, a less comprehensive version of NEPA, was cosponsored by all but one member of Dingell's subcommittee. This bill authorized the establishment of an executive council for the environment, which would discuss matters of environmental management and prepare an annual report. Dingell's bill also contained a statement detailing a national environmental policy, although it was much shorter and weaker than what was finally adopted. Dingell's bill contained no "action-forcing" mechanism requiring the preparation of environmental impact statements. However, between the third and fourth sessions of congressional hearings on H.R. 6750, Congressman Lucien Nedzi introduced H.R. 12143, which contained requirements for investigative environmental findings. This proposal was referred to Dingell's subcommittee.[17] H.R. 12143 was important because Dingell's bill had no "findings" requirement. In executive session, the Subcommittee on Fisheries and Wildlife Conservation created the compromise bill, H.R. 12549. This was reported by the entire Merchant Marine and Fisheries Committee on July 11, 1969, and reached the House floor on September 23.

However, before the measure could be considered by the House, a ruling was required from the Rules Committee to establish the parameters of the debate. Here, the bill ran into trouble. Congressman Wayne Aspinall (D-Colo.), chairman of the House Interior and Insular Affairs Committee and member of the House Rules Committee, raised objections about the jurisdictional ramifications of Dingell's bill. The work of reorganizing the maze of federal programs was in fact a continuation of the work already being done by the Public Land Law Review Commission chaired by Congressman Aspinall.

Aspinall voiced concerns over the supposed vagueness of the bill and sought to clarify exactly how the measure was to be applied and how the existing authority of federal agencies would be affected. He also believed that H.R. 6750 should not be exclusively under the domain of the Fish and Wildlife Committee, as environmental policy was too broad a topic to be under the oversight of a single House committee. Aspinall was a strong supporter of resource development and he naturally wanted to protect both his own political agenda and his committee's position in the creation of environmental policy. Aspinall was also concerned with the opaqueness of the word "environment" as well as the potential jurisdictional problems caused by H.R. 6750.[18] Congressman Aspinall feared NEPA's provisions would provide new tools for environmentalists to obstruct natural resource development. Because of Aspinall's influence on the House Rules Committee, Dingell was forced to accept Aspinall's amendments to the proposed legislation. The first amendment erased all references to the Fish and Wildlife Coordination Act. The second amendment added the "no change" disclaimer (sec. 9): "Nothing in this Act shall increase, decrease, or change any responsibility or authority of any Federal official or agency created by other provision of law."[19]

On May 29, 1969, during the hearings for Dingell's H.R. 6750, President Nixon issued an executive order creating a cabinet-level environmental quality council. This action complicated congressional initiatives for establishing an environmental council and necessitated revisions in Congress's statutory proposals.[20] Nixon's environmental council would have included Vice President Spiro Agnew as vice chair and the secretaries of agriculture; commerce; housing and urban development; the interior; transportation; and health, education, and welfare. President Nixon argued that this council would "provide the focal point for this Administration's efforts to protect all of our natural resources." Specifically, he saw the council's job as coordinating a governmental attack on all forms of pollution. Nixon stated that this would include addressing the threats to "the availability of good air and good water, of open space and even quiet neighborhoods."[21]

Despite the president's environmental rhetoric, both Dingell and Jackson had grave misgivings about the abilities and inherent limitations of an interagency council; they preferred a more independent council housed outside the White House cabinet. Several commentators who testified before the House Committee on Merchant Marine and Fisheries agreed with Dingell's and Jackson's concerns, asserting that such a council would catalyze the pitfalls of "group thinking."[22] A council of internal political cronies would internalize a noncritical discourse of "yes men." Charles Callison, then executive director of the National Audubon Society, further explained this concern: "There is a natural human tendency by all the members of such an interagency council to be good fellows, have a meeting and decide we will run our program in our department and you will run yours and we will take a quick look at these programs and then perhaps make a few adjustments. But they never really come to grips with the genuine problems that have arisen in these programs."[23]

Senators Muskie and Jackson, among others, thought the president's proposal was an ineffective "patchwork approach" to environmental problems, which was "little better than nothing."[24] It was the opinion of Jackson, Muskie, Dingell, and other key participants in NEPA's formation that Congress's CEQ version would be less prone to administrative favoritism, wrangling, and biases toward, for example, economic considerations over environmental impacts. They favored an executive council, created by legislative action, to put environmental decision making in the hands of a diversified group of environmental experts who were not bound by political ties and constraints.[25]

In an executive session of his subcommittee, Dingell created H.R. 12549, the revised version of H.R. 6750. This revised bill was essentially the same as the H.R. 6750 that had been reported by the Merchant Marine and Fisheries Committee on July 11, 1969. In the only roll call vote on NEPA, the

House passed H.R. 12549 by a vote of 372 to 15 with 43 abstentions.[26] Those in opposition to the bill were conservatives, primarily from the South and Midwest. These included Congressman Jamie Whitten (D-Miss.), chairman of the Appropriations Committee, and Congressman William Scherle (R-Iowa), two individuals who eventually would oversee the CEQ budget.[27]

The CEQ Debate

The CEQ's provisions were essentially to oversee the implementation of NEPA and to provide environmental advice to the president and Congress. This meant providing guidelines for federal agencies to follow in the preparation of environmental impact statements. CEQ was also to be a forecaster of environmental trends, and in that capacity was to report to the president and publish an annual report detailing the state of the environment.[28]

The organizational structure of the CEQ was constantly debated in NEPA's formative process. President Nixon wanted to establish a small board with the White House in full control. Dingell and Jackson wanted the CEQ to be big enough to be able to sufficiently monitor the condition of the environment. They feared the new executive council would lack the power and resources it would need. Nixon said the CEQ measure provided "an adequate organization" and consequently there was no need for additional executive staffing concerning the environment.[29] Through interrogating administrative officials at the Senate Interior and Insular Affairs Committee hearing on S. 1075, committee members learned that Nixon's "proposed cabinet council would have little or no full-time staff support."[30] Congressional squabbling eventually led to a jurisdictional dispute between Muskie and Jackson and among several House members, which held up action on both bills. Finally, after some late-night negotiating, Muskie was assured that Jackson's Senate bill 1075 provision for a CEQ would complement the details for a CEQ as laid out in Muskie's Senate bill 7.

The argument for "another" CEQ also complicated congressional efforts to pass a statutory CEQ. Republican congressmen, following the lead of their administration, lamented over how unnecessary they thought a differently structured executive office was and argued that it would simply cause further bureaucratic tangles and confusion. The secretary of the interior, Walter Hickel, argued that Nixon's newly established Environmental Quality Council, chaired by the president with members and staff from various departments and careers, "makes unnecessary the kind of Council proposed by S. 1075. . . . It is our recommendation that legislation such as that contained in Title I of S. 1075 not be enacted until the new council has had full opportunity to address itself to this need."[31]

However, the intentions and structure of President Nixon's proposed interagency council were very different from the executive council proposed by S. 1075. As Caldwell said to the Senate committee, the council created by S. 1075 would not be another ad hoc administrative body; rather, "It is intended to provide for the independent review of the existing environmental state of the country . . . [and] can be counted upon to provide the inputs of time and attention to raise the difficult and inconvenient questions."[32]

The creators of NEPA placed the CEQ within the executive office of the president, rather than in the cabinet, to facilitate rigorous oversight and enforcement that was not as dependent on interagency politics.[33] It was important to avoid "groupthink," a situation in which group members tend not to think and act as independently as they might otherwise, due to their preconceived perceptions of other members and, particularly, the president. Caldwell noted:

> If we have such a Council there are going to be times when there is going to be friction. Such a Council is going to have before it findings and reports which heads of Executive Agencies will not like. [Yet] maybe these are considerations that at least ought to have an airing, ought to be discussed. It seems to me much more likely that they will be discussed in this independent Council than they will be discussed if you have a Council composed of Cabinet officers who, out of courtesy to one another, or concern for the troubles of their fellow Cabinet officers, are not going to make their own life more difficult.[34]

The Muskie-Jackson Compromise

Before Dingell's House bill and Jackson's Senate bill could go to the conference committee where the bills would be molded into one piece of legislation, Jackson first needed to settle a jurisdictional conflict with Maine senator Edmund Muskie. Senator Jackson, chief sponsor of S. 1075, chaired the Senate Interior and Insular Affairs Committee, while Senator Muskie chaired the Air and Water Pollution Subcommittee of the Senate Public Works Committee.

On June 12, 1969, Muskie, with forty cosponsors, introduced an amendment to the Omnibus Water Pollution Control Bill (S. 7) being considered by his committee. This amendment, S. 2391, was the first evidence in the public record that clearly showed Muskie's concern for the jurisdictional problems created by S. 1075.[35] Specifically, Muskie feared that Jackson's measure would debilitate the existing environmental goals and programs of his Air and Water Pollution Subcommittee. Muskie and others on his committee thought that agencies with nonenvironmental concerns, such as the transportation sector, could not be trusted to follow a new course of action that mandated the consideration of environmental impacts. Muskie agreed with the requirement directing federal agencies to disclose their environmental findings (the "formal finding" clause). But he argued that this was insufficient because there were no outside review provisions.

Muskie was troubled with the "formal finding" clause essentially because he questioned whether such findings would be subject to serious scrutiny from other agencies, Congress, or the public. Further, given wide discretion, Muskie believed agencies with a vested interest in depleting environmental quality would not report in the most reliable fashion. Muskie explained his feelings on the Senate floor in 1969: "The concept of self-policing by Federal agencies which pollute or license pollution is contrary to the philosophy and intent of existing environmental quality legislation."[36] Senator Muskie accurately foresaw many obstacles that environmental policy—and specifically NEPA—would face, especially within agencies whose very mission involves environmental degradation.

Muskie called for some outside checking or review of agency decisions. In order to garner outside comments and reviews, Muskie insisted that copies of the "detailed statement" or "formal finding" be circulated among other appropriate agencies (federal, state, and local), as well as interested citizens and interest groups. This was obviously to ensure the continued powers of environmental agencies and committees that already existed—including those under Senator Muskie's jurisdiction. NEPA's section 103 was also added. It explained that the preparation of environmental impact statements would not change the existing authorizations and obligations of federal agencies to comply with other environmental laws and quality standards.[37]

Senator Jackson argued that requiring a "detailed statement" should be applicable to "all agencies that have responsibilities that affect the environment."[38] Interestingly, Senator Muskie believed that air and water pollution regulations should be exempt from such a requirement. He apparently feared that Jackson's S. 1075 would engulf and usurp environmental programs for which Muskie's subcommittee had jurisdiction.

Muskie and Jackson's differences also derived from contrasting beliefs over environmental management procedures and models. Muskie's desire for outside review also seemed to suggest a call for outside sanctioning and enforcing mechanisms, such as public opinion, public-interest lawsuits, judicial review, and criticism from other agencies. In sum, Muskie was concerned that even though federal agencies were to be fully informed of the environmental effects of their proposals, they would still be left with the ultimate choice as to how and whether to commence with proposed remedial or lower-impact action. He was, as we have since learned, correct.

Today, as long as an agency complies with the EIS procedural requirements in NEPA, final decisions on whether to proceed with the proposed action are left up to the agency. This is problematic because many agencies interacting with the environment are geared primarily toward the pursuit of economic and other goals unrelated to environmental protection. Furthermore, internal agency decision-making processes often precast the outcome of possible agency choices. For instance, the Forest Service is often criticized by environmentalists as being so thoroughly dominated by logging interests that forests are looked upon as nothing more than tree farms. National forests are eulogized euphemistically as "aged specimens" requiring "even-age management"—in other words, agricultural products to be harvested so as to maximize political and economic benefits. In such a political context, the parameters structuring the negotiation processes are drawn to fit the interests of the respective agency's jurisdiction, and the outcome of the decision-making process is all but predetermined.

Unlike the resolution of House committee disagreements, by allowing Congressman Wayne Aspinall (D-Colo.) a place on the conference committee, no members of Muskie's Public Works Committee were appointed as conferees on S. 1075. Thus, Muskie was left to work out his differences with Jackson's S. 1075 before the conference committee met. Four important modifications of S. 1075 were made with regard to the EIS process. First, the requirement in section 102(c) for a "formal finding" of the environmental impacts was changed to a "detailed statement." Second, a measure was added to make statements widely available and to require consultation with environmental agencies when developing an environmental impact statement. The consulting language had the profound effect of instigating an external review process that thereby improved environmental accountability and helped to reduce arbitrary and capricious bureaucratic decision making. Third, section 103 was added, delineating the continued obligation of federal agencies to comply with other existing federal laws. This statement resolved Muskie's concern that air and water pollution laws would play second fiddle to Jackson's NEPA. Fourth, the language of section 303 was amended to require that the president's annual environmental quality report be submitted to all congressional committees having jurisdiction over the environment.[39]

To bring policies and practices that impact the environment under some sort of similar rule and to balance the countervailing interests among the agencies and between Jackson and Muskie, the environmental assessment requirements were created. This aspect of NEPA was heavily influenced by Caldwell's idea for the environmental impact statement. Because of the Muskie-Jackson compromise, the amended version of Senate Bill 1075 was easily approved. On October 8, 1969, it was presented to the Senate during deliberation of Muskie's water pollution control bill. It was agreed that the revised S. 1075 be negotiated with House Resolution 12549 (formerly 6750) in the conference committee.

NEPA in the House-Senate Conference

Following the political jockeying that fashioned the Muskie-Jackson compromise, as well as the Dingell-Aspinall agreement, the final form of NEPA was settled in the House-Senate conference committee. Representing the House were Aspinall, Dingell, Edward Garmatz (D-Md.), William S. Mailliard (R-Calif.), and John Saylor (R-Pa.). Representing the Senate were Gordon L. Allott (R-Colo.), Frank Church (D-Idaho), Jackson, Len Jordan

(R-Idaho), and Gaylord Nelson (D-Wisc.), all from the Senate's Interior and Insular Affairs Committee. The unique inclusion of Aspinall and Saylor (two representatives from other House committees) was a result of the Dingell-Aspinall compromise. The conference considered H.R. 12549, S. 1075 in its original form, and S. 1075 as revised by the Muskie-Jackson compromise. Three views were represented at the conference: the Senate conferees under Jackson, the House conferees controlled by Dingell, and Congressman Aspinall who was a part of the conference by the special agreement between Dingell and Aspinall.

The opening sentence of the Senate report to the Joint Conference on a National Policy for the Environment set the tone: "It is the unanimous view of the members of the Interior and Insular Affairs Committee that our Nation's present state of knowledge, our established public policies, and our existing governmental institutions are not adequate to deal with the growing environmental problems and crises the Nation faces." NEPA eventually changed this conundrum—on the legislative level at least. As the Senate report clearly documents, NEPA's "purpose is to establish, by congressional action, a national policy to guide federal activities which are involved with or related to the management of the environment or which have an impact on the quality of the environment."[40]

Two issues were raised during the conference that would have a significant impact on the long-term prospects for strong federal environmental protection. The first was the deletion of Jackson's provision that every citizen has a "right [to a] healthful environment." The environmental rights provision was eliminated because of fear that this might give constitutional power to environmentalists and their interest groups to aggressively pursue such newly created "rights" in the courts.[41]

The second important change emerging from the conference committee involved the structuring of section 102 in Title I of Senator Jackson's S. 1075. This change, under the influence of Congressman Aspinall, involved two related aspects. First, the requirement that federal agencies' procedures for evaluating unquantifiable environmental values be approved by the CEQ was deleted. This was changed to what now is section 102(2)(B), which simply requires agencies to consult with the CEQ when constructing such procedures. The second factor involved rearranging the placement of the words "to the fullest extent possible." Again, Aspinall objected to the compromise Muskie-Jackson version of S. 1075 because it appeared to be too strong and potentially disruptive to the status quo. Section 102 originally read, "The Congress authorizes and directs that the policies, regulations, and public laws of the United States, to the fullest extent possible, be interpreted and administered in accordance with the policies set forth in this Act." Aspinall's suggestion served to strengthen the "policies, regulations, and public laws" clause. The altered language, which was later passed as the final version of NEPA, reads: "The Congress authorizes and directs that, to the fullest extent possible: (1) the policies, regulations, and public laws of the United States shall be interpreted and administered in accordance with the policies set forth in this Act."[42]

This argument was crucial because some agencies would seek to limit their responsibility under the new act. For example, the Atomic Energy Commission (AEC, the licensing and regulatory functions of which are now under the Nuclear Regulatory Commission) argued that the thermal pollution caused by nuclear power plants was an issue beyond its jurisdiction.[43] The AEC's shifting of bureaucratic responsibilities was not an isolated incident in the federal departments and agencies. Given the disparate power bases in the bureaucracy, a unifying mechanism was needed to ensure that environmental considerations were taken seriously by all federal agencies. In the end, the conference committee did make it clear that "nothing in the bill altered the statutory responsibilities of any federal agency."[44] The final language in the bill granted "authority to every federal agency to implement the environmental policy act as part of its established responsibilities."[45]

Aspinall's position on the conference committee allowed him to argue, not entirely persuasively, for the "no change in responsibility clause." The "fullest extent possible" change was accepted by the conferees in return for the elimination of Aspinall's "no change in authority" amendment, which would have essentially gutted the main intentions behind the Dingell and Jackson bills. According to Daniel Dreyfus and Helen Ingram, had "this provision not been modified by conference and its effect mitigated by the language of the conference report, this amendment would have negated [NEPA's] action-forcing mechanism." The statement of the House managers explained this: "It is the intent of the conferees that the provision 'to the fullest extent possible' shall not be used by any Federal agency as a means of avoiding compliance with the directions set out in Section 102.

. . . No agency shall utilize any excessively narrow construction of its existing statutory authorizations to avoid compliance."[46]

The final bill delineated in the conference committee report was passed by a voice vote in the Senate on December 20, and similarly by the House on December 22, clearing the way for the president's signature twelve days later.[47]

Nixon Signs NEPA into Law

On January 1, 1970, President Nixon enacted his first major piece of legislation of the new decade when he signed S. 1075, the final version of NEPA, in a ceremony held at the White House.[48] Nixon sanguinely proclaimed the 1970s as the environmental decade, whereby "America pays its debts to the past by reclaiming the purity of its air, its waters, and our living environment." Nixon warned, "It is literally now or never."[49]

Although only a few highly involved participants realized it at the time, NEPA was about to make major institutional changes and fundamental reforms throughout the federal bureaucracy. A very readable and concise document, NEPA was a relatively radical and unusual step forward in public policy making—especially environmental policy. Most congressional legislation is incremental in nature.[50] In that respect NEPA is philosophically and procedurally very different from most legislation. With a profound—and ambitious—national environmental policy statement, NEPA mandated the wholesale rearranging of institutional decision making within federal agencies. Agencies were now held accountable for the environment on which their decisions had an impact.

NEPA created a law that significantly expanded the boundaries of regulation and institutional arrangements with respect to the environment. As a whole, NEPA broke new ground in environmental policy. Four areas are most important. First, NEPA declared a national philosophy and specific goals for the environment that did not previously exist. Second, the law provided an administrative tool for ensuring consideration of environmental ramifications resulting from federal agency actions. Third, NEPA provided a legal ground via the Administrative Procedures Act (APA) for citizen suits if NEPA's procedures are not properly followed by the agencies. Fourth, NEPA created an executive coordinating office for the natural environment: NEPA Title II created the Council on Environmental Quality to collect data and track environmental statistics and to make recommendations to the president regarding environmental policy.

Despite the resulting flood of scholarly writings, judicial battles, and regulatory adjustments, NEPA was hardly noticed by the major news media when the act was passed by Congress. The *New York Times* on January 2, 1970, noted the establishment of new environmental reporting requirements and their headline framed Senator Jackson as "Sponsor of Pollution Control Bill."[51] At the time of its passage, NEPA was not controversial legislation. Environmental interest groups and their lobbyists were aware of the bill but were not actively pressing for its passage.[52]

Because environmental issues created a new constituency in the late 1960s and 1970s, there were political points to be won by politicians of every stripe by supporting environmental legislation. NEPA moved through the legislative process on an early but substantial wave of environmental concern. A window of opportunity existed for environmental policy. There were few federal environmental laws of any scope and no coherent national environmental policy. Consequently, legislators, particularly NEPA's founders and sponsors, eagerly worked to pass a national environmental law to fill this policy void.

Conclusion

Senator Jackson characterized NEPA in 1969 as "the most important and far-reaching environmental and conservation measure ever enacted."[53] The legislative history of NEPA, from its ideological roots to its policy design and statutory language, is interesting and full of political nuances calling attention to the multifaceted dynamics of public policy making. Bargaining, trade-offs, and credit-claiming are all characteristics of policy making that influenced the final version of NEPA. NEPA would soon be subjected to narrow legal interpretation and presidential and agency indifference. Taken together, these have withered substantial parts and purposes of NEPA.

President Nixon's involvement with NEPA illustrates this political paradox. Although President Nixon attempted to garner maximum political gain and attention from signing NEPA, the Nixon administration aggressively opposed passage of any NEPA measure throughout its legislative history. Reviewing NEPA congressional hearings, it is clear that Nixon wanted some administrative changes—including an office of environmental quality in the executive branch. Nixon's motives appear to reflect a desire for more control in the executive office, rather than any philosophical principles of ecological harmony as espoused in Title I of NEPA. In fact, Dreyfus and Ingram describe Nixon's signature on January 1, 1970, as "a belated and lukewarm acquiescence to growing national concern with the environment."[54]

As its main sponsor, Jackson had great hopes for NEPA. Caldwell, Jackson, and Muskie all envisioned NEPA as a statute that embraced and supported comprehensive environmental responsibility on the part of federal agencies. NEPA was created to address fragmented and disjointed conditions for environmental accountability. Originally, NEPA not only mandated a more inclusive and comprehensive planning design but also required federal projects to be developed within the environmental goals of section 101. This was the intention and philosophy of NEPA. What it is today, at least as implemented, is something else—side-stepped by agencies, courts, and presidents.

CHAPTER 4

NEPA Policy Goals: Ecology and Administration

T he three fundamental parts of NEPA discussed in this chapter are (1) its explicit declaration of a national policy for the environment detailing a uniform set of ideals, goals, and agendas for all those involved with environmental policy making (sec. 101); (2) a directive to all federal agencies to carry out investigative procedures, and the "action-forcing mechanism" (secs. 102–105) for projects that significantly affect the environment; and (3) establishment of the Council on Environmental Quality (Title II). We also examine the debates over how the entire statute and its sections have come to be interpreted, implemented, and enforced by federal agencies and federal courts.

The Nexus between Science and Politics

The goals of NEPA's authors, even if they had survived the subsequent policy-making process of formulations, administrative regulations, and judicial interpretations of the act, might well have been very difficult to achieve under the best of circumstances. Above all, the success and the failures of NEPA can be better understood if one has an appreciation of the relationship between scientific analysis and the policy process. For example, it is one thing to provide Americans with the legislative goals of a clean and healthy environment; it is another to determine what constitutes a clean and healthy environment and translate that determination into public policy. The development and passage of NEPA, like any environmental legislation, involves the integration of science into politics and the policy-making process. Turning science into policy via a political system that utilizes bargaining, compromise, and incremental decision making is not easy.

A number of problems are associated with the use of science in policy making. Some of these are problems for the policy maker, whereas others are problems for the scientist. From the perspective of the policy maker, scientific information is often not delivered in neat, usable bundles that are readily adaptable to the policy problems at hand. As former Colorado governor Richard Lamm put it, "I find that the scientific community has a tendency to formulate problems narrowly—to have a specialized tunnel vision which does not see or fully appreciate all the public policy factors of a decision."[1] Scientific input into the policy-making process often suffers from the hammer-and-nail syndrome: If all you have is a hammer, the whole world looks like a nail. The specificity and specialization required of science may not be conducive to the comprehensiveness and generalizability needed in policy formation. Quite naturally, a biologist might first think of ecosystem problems in terms of species populations. In contrast, a chemist might think of the chemical properties of the air or water in the ecosystem.

The second problem has to do with the different currencies used in politics and in science. Politics is about bargaining, compromise, and the balancing of interests. In addition, economics, particularly cost-benefit analysis, plays an important, often central, role in policy formation. Science, on the other hand, tries to deal in "truth," that is, to the extent possible, absolutes. The scientifically correct solution to a problem may not be politically viable.[2] The EIS process assumes, in part, that decision making in bureaucracies is a comprehensive and rational process that relies on analysis of all available information. NEPA attempts to require bringing more ecological and social information into rational calculation. But, as P. H. Friesema and P. J. Culhane, like others, have attested, "Public administration behavior is not scientific management, it is politics."[3]

Douglas Amy has asserted that an EIS may even have the unintended consequence of legitimating unsustainable agency actions: "Instead of guiding decisions, the EIS becomes a way of retrospectively rationalizing and legitimatizing, decisions made on other grounds. . . . For administrators, then, what is often politically useful about the EIS is not that it increases the rationality of their decisions—but that it enhances the *appearance* of rationality and thus serves to undermine environmental opposition to development projects."[4] A final problem in the relationship between science and policy formation has particular pertinence for NEPA. Scientists themselves seem to prefer certainty or the perception of certainty in the face of qualification.

Thus there is often a presumption that environmental policy-making decisions should not be made without all the available information at hand. Furthermore, it is argued, decisions should not be made about the environment unless the scientific evidence establishes clear causality, without uncertainty, and is direct and provable. Yet science is not well suited to providing this kind of evidence. The standard of certainty and unquestioned causality is, in fact, rarely met in science. Scientific conclusions are often necessarily drawn from the probabilities of a particular outcome. Nonscientific policy makers (whether legislators, executives, or bureaucrats) do not seem to understand this about science, and often demand "hard scientific fact" before proceeding to a policy conclusion. As Wade Robison has written, "In fact we are never in a position to know, regarding any environmental matter of any moment, that we have all the relevant information. Requiring that we have all relevant information thus sets up a heuristic ideal, powering continual demands for more information and thus for more research."[5] The call for more information and research, while a worthwhile goal, is used to derail preventive policy from being drafted. President Ronald Reagan's continued thwarting of solutions to environmental problems with the call for more research is testimony to Robinson's argument.

Paul Feyerabend addressed scientists encouraging this expectation in his scathing critique of contemporary science: "Unanimity is often the result of a *political* decision: dissenters are suppressed, or remain silent to preserve the reputation of science as a source of trustworthy, almost infallible knowledge. On other occasions, unanimity is the result of shared prejudices: positions are taken without detailed examination of the matter under review and are infused with the same authority which proceeds from detailed research."[6]

Finally, some, in policy making and outside, are skeptical of science. People who know little about probability are fond of saying that "statistics lie." Policy makers have, when confronted with scientific evidence that is contrary to their political ideals, simply dismissed scientific contributions out of hand. Research on global warming, for example, has regularly been criticized, when not ignored, by representatives of the fossil fuel industry and their supporters in the U.S. Congress.[7]

Some have also argued that research priorities are skewed, given that most research is carried out for purposes of profit, often defense profits, or social control.[8] Most research is driven by corporate and government priorities—the defense industry is a prominent example; much of the work in computing, climate, and materials engineering is funded by the military. As Brian Martin has written, "The priorities for ostensibly 'pure' research are often influenced by government and corporate priorities. [An] example is high-energy physics, an indirect beneficiary of the priority placed on nuclear weapons and nuclear power."[9] Both research and development, in areas from pharmaceuticals to pesticides, are driven by corporate priorities and profits. Although many in the scientific community would argue that scientific research can be carried out objectively regardless of the source of funding, there is little question that research priorities can lead us down one environmental path as opposed to another. For example, more money is spent on figuring out how to mitigate the negative effects of existing technological adaptations—such as the internal combustion engine—than on creating completely new and ecologically sustainable technologies.

NEPA was an attempt by Congress to circumvent this type of poor planning. One very significant contribution to decision making was NEPA's requirement of interdisciplinary science and analysis. In *Baltimore Gas and Electric Company v. Natural Resources Defense Council, Inc.* (462 U.S. 97, 1983) the Supreme Court declared that NEPA has two primary purposes. The first aim is to create "an obligation to consider every significant aspect of the environmental impact of a proposed action." The second goal, according to the Court, is to ensure "that the agency will inform the public that it has considered environmental concerns in its decision-making process."

NEPA Declaration and Statement of Intention

In many ways, section 101 of NEPA is remarkable testimony to the ecological foresight of NEPA's authors. In 1993 Dinah Bear, general counsel to the Council on Environmental Quality, stated, "biological diversity, recycling, future generational rights, and sustainable development are all hot issues on today's environmental agenda, and all were presaged by NEPA's authors."[10] Like Bear's, our observation of NEPA as an ecological model clearly substantiates the language of the Senate committee responsible for NEPA's creation. The Senate Committee on Interior and Insular Affairs explicitly explained the broad purpose of section 101: "[Section 101] is a declaration by the Congress of a national environmental policy. The declaration is based upon a congressional recognition of mankind's dependence upon his physical and biological surroundings for material goods and cultural enrichment. It is further based upon a recognition of the increasing pressures exerted upon the environment as a result of population growth, urbanization, industrial expansion, resource exploitation, and technological development."[11] Indeed, section 101(b) commands the federal government to use all practicable means, consistent with other essential considerations of national policy, to

(i) fulfill the responsibilities of each generation as trustee of the environment for succeeding generations;
(ii) assure for all Americans safe, healthful, productive, and aesthetically and culturally pleasing surroundings;
(iii) attain the widest range of beneficial uses of the environment without degradation, risk to health or safety, or any other undesirable or unintended consequences;
(iv) preserve important historic, cultural, and natural aspects of our national heritage, and maintain, wherever possible, an environment which supports diversity, and variety of individual choice;
(v) achieve a balance between population and resource use which will permit high standards of living and a wide sharing of life's amenities; and
(vi) enhance the quality of renewable resources and approach the maximum attainable recycling of depletable resources.[12]

The declared purposes of this act are cast in a remarkable, holistic tone of ecological insight: "The purposes of the Act are: to declare a national policy which will encourage productive and enjoyable harmony between [humans] and [the] environment; to promote efforts which will prevent or eliminate damage to the environment and biosphere and stimulate the health and welfare of [humans]; to enrich the understanding of the ecological systems and natural resources important to the Nation; and to establish a Council of Environmental Quality."[13]

Section 101(a) in Title I sets forth additional goals and purposes of this legislation: "The Congress, recognizing the profound impact of [humans'] activity on the interrelations of all components of the natural environment, . . . [directs] the Federal Government to . . . foster and promote the general welfare, to create and maintain conditions under which [humans] and nature can exist in productive harmony, and fulfill the social, economic, and other requirements of present and future generations of Americans." Congress declared that the federal government would cooperate to these ends with "State and local governments, and other concerned public and private organizations, to use all practicable means and measures, including financial and technical assistance."[14]

It is clear from section 101's language and the act's legislative history, that Congress intended to enact an environmental law that would ensure the creation and maintenance of a harmonious and interconnected relationship between humans and the nonhuman world of nature. This was the ecophilosophy, the "ecological rationality" driving NEPA.[15] It was also the part of NEPA first dismissed by the courts as unenforceable and consequently never completely enforced by federal agencies.

Yet these congressional intentions are important because they provide the foundation for NEPA's substantive purposes. The legislative history of NEPA reveals that the authors did not intend for the EIS process to be simply another hurdle agencies must jump over before they carry on with whatever agenda they had already envisioned or planned. Yet a CEQ study of NEPA implementation published in 1997 found that "agencies sometimes confuse the purpose of NEPA." Kathleen McGinty, chair of CEQ, concluded that agencies often act "as if the detailed statement called for in the statute is an end in itself, rather than a tool to enhance and improve decision making."[16]

The Environmental Impact Statement:
NEPA's Action-Forcing Section

NEPA's section 102 was constructed out of many compromises and amendments. Neither the original Senate bill 1075 nor H.R. 6750 contained any environmental impact statement provisions. Like Jackson's S.1075, Dingell's proposal included only a brief policy statement, a requirement for an annual report, and the establishment of the CEQ. Congress eventually decided it would require agencies to implement NEPA's substantive policy recommendations through the "action-forcing" procedures of section 102. NEPA's authors recognized a lack of environmental accountability and proposed a new set of ecological commandments, along with mechanisms to implement the new planning considerations and policy goals.

During NEPA's formation, Caldwell, addressing the urgency of environmental responsibility, contended that "Congress should at least consider measures to require the Federal agencies, in submitting proposals, to contain with the proposals an evaluation of the effect of these proposals upon the state of the environment."[17] Indeed, Senator Jackson came to envision the EIS process as a mechanism for regulating federal agencies in a comprehensive way within the preexisting institutional structures. This enforcement tool would be universally applied across bureaucratic jurisdictions. Jackson articulated the importance of this sort of unifying mechanism in a floor speech where he argued for the Senate version of the legislation that established the EIS procedure. Jackson declared: "There are about eighty major Federal agencies with programs under way which affect the quality of the human environment. If environmental policy is to become more than rhetoric, and if the studies and advice of any high-level advisory group are to be translated into action, each of these agencies must be enabled and directed to participate in active and objective-oriented environmental management."[18] Based on their past record, agencies could not be trusted simply to act forthwith on the ethical principles of Title I. As Douglas J. Amy explained:

> The reasoning behind the EIS requirement was simple and appealing. [For] too long had the nation been recklessly building highways,

filling in wetlands, cutting down forests, and damming rivers with little concern for the long-range environmental effects. Now officials would be required to "look before they leap." And the hope was that now that officials were equipped with more information and more options they would be able to make better (i.e., more scientific and rational) decisions that would minimize environmental damage.[19]

Jackson said NEPA's substantive environmental policy would "serve a constitutional function in that people may refer to it for guidance in making decisions where environmental values are found to be in conflict with other values."[20] In sum, the EIS mandate was intended to ensure the full incorporation of Title I in federal decisions.

Caldwell's ideas were ultimately incorporated into NEPA's sections 102–105. Thus it came about that the policy provisions in section 101 were to be supported by section 102's action-forcing procedure, which "authorizes and directs that, to the fullest extent possible, the policies and regulations and laws of the United States shall be interpreted and administered in accordance with the policies . . . in this Act."[21] Of course, "to the fullest extent possible" has come to mean many different things to different agency administrators (and often has no effect whatsoever). The courts have left this decision largely up to the discretion of agencies and their respective expertise, thereby complicating the enforcement of NEPA's environmental policy goals.

To determine whether there are conflicts between environmental quality and agency proposals, "all agencies of the Federal Government shall" utilize a thorough, "systematic, interdisciplinary approach" to prepare a "detailed statement" of the environmental impacts of any proposed "legislation and other major Federal actions significantly affecting the quality of the human environment."[22] This central feature of NEPA requires that

1. "environmental amenities and values be given appropriate consideration in decision making, along with economic and technical considerations";
2. decision makers "recognize the worldwide and long-range character of environmental problems";
3. decision makers explore all the "appropriate alternatives";

4. agencies "make available" to a wide audience the proposed plan of action; and

5. agencies seek and share "advice and information useful in restoring, maintaining, and enhancing the quality of the environment," and "initiate and utilize ecological information in the planning and development of resource-oriented projects."[23]

The "detailed statement" is to include: "(i) the environmental impact of the proposed action, (ii) any adverse environmental effects which cannot be avoided should the proposal be implemented, (iii) alternatives to the proposed action, (iv) the relationship between local and short-term uses of man's environment and the maintenance and enhancement of long-term productivity, and (v) any irreversible and irretrievable commitments of resources which would be involved in the proposed action should it be implemented."[24] Thus federal officials are explicitly required to consider the environmental impact of their proposed projects. It is the intention of NEPA's language that if federal officials have accurate information on environmental impact, their decisions should reflect this information.[25] Clearly, completely ignoring ecological effects violates NEPA's intent.

The EIS as an information-gathering device is one of the most common ways of understanding the act. In many ways, this method of understanding NEPA is more technical than political; decision making is understood as a rational-scientific process, rather than a pluralist, negotiated process. In theory, knowledge is to be quantified and plugged into the cybernetic, apolitical decision-making model and the "correct" decision will emerge. In fact, most articles in the *Impact Assessment Bulletin* and the *Environmental Impact Assessment Review*, two NEPA trade journals, tend to emphasize technical aspects of gathering, organizing, and utilizing information from specialists and experts, as well as the public.

Of course, adequate information-gathering mechanisms for NEPA are of utmost importance to all those involved with its implementation.[26] But in fact, however, as economic-based cost-benefit analysis has become more and more in vogue, important qualitative environmental data often get buried in the minutiae of narrow economic criteria. Julian Dunster brashly asserted that information concerning environmental impact is generally considered "better quantitative and wrong than qualitative and right." Yet NEPA should be understood as a document that encourages organizations to think so qualitatively and ecologically as to obviate the EIS in the first place.[27]

Linking NEPA Sections 101 and 102

Section 101 of Title I establishes a national philosophy to preserve and protect the environment. Environmental impact analysis seeks to shape internal planning and decision making by anticipating and mitigating social, environmental, cultural, economic, and other impacts. NEPA charges all federal agencies with upholding its philosophy in following their respective mandates as set forth in section 102. Focusing particularly on the EIS requirement, Culhane, Friesema, and Beecher defined it as the "internal reform" model.[28] The new national policy for the environment articulated by NEPA was intended to be implemented as a vehicle for aggressive and progressive federal action.

The goals of the new policies as set forth in section 101 were to be directly incorporated into the bureaucratic and regulatory decision-making systems. The prescriptions set forth in section 102 were intended to implement the lofty declarations and goals that section 101 addressed. Section 102 was written to overcome problems in enforcing these requirements. It is important to note this because the ends-based goals of section 101 are also the goals underlying NEPA's procedural mandate, section 102. The established link between these two sections was explicitly written into the statute. As section 102(1) states, "the policies, regulations, and public laws of the United States shall be interpreted and administered in accordance with the policies set forth in this Act."[29]

The Senate Committee on Interior and Insular Affairs explained the reasoning behind the intentional marriage of the substantive provisions of section 101 to the procedural requirements of section 102:

> The policies and goals set forth in section 101 can be implemented if they are incorporated into the ongoing activities of the Federal Government in carrying out its responsibilities to the public. In many areas of Federal action there is no body of experience or precedent for substantial and consistent consideration of environmental factors in decision

making. In some areas of Federal activity, existing legislation does not provide clear authority for the consideration of environmental factors [that] . . . conflict with other objectives. To remedy present shortcomings in the legislative foundation . . . pro-action-forcing procedures will help to insure that the policies enunciated in section 101 are implemented.[30]

Section 102 details the procedures by which federal agencies are to explore, implement, or at least include environmental considerations in their decision-making process. This is done through a detailed interdisciplinary statement. Now commonly known as the environmental impact statement, this has emerged as the best known and most litigated element of NEPA. This operative, action-forcing mechanism of NEPA is directed primarily at departments, bureaus, and agencies of the federal government, although individuals, corporations, and state and local governments are also frequently involved in the process via their direct partnerships with federal agencies.

Institutionalizing the policies and goals of NEPA was not necessarily going to be uniform, because the intersections between federal agencies and the environment were too diverse to lend themselves to being managed by a single monolithic bureaucratic process or entity. That is also why Congress had to delegate some responsibility to the federal agencies themselves for properly implementing NEPA.

However, as in the case of NEPA and the respective implementing agencies, changing bureaucratic structures is not easy. Hanna Cortner contended that NEPA's requirements for organizational restructuring were not willingly accepted in many agencies. Cortner identified several contributing factors in this resistance: "These characteristics include the bureaucratic organization's constricted communications structure, its flow and use of information, its basic quest for institutional survival, its statutory mission and financial incentives to perform that mandate, its negotiated accommodations with clientele groups, its support from staff, consultants, and sister agencies, and its capabilities in terms of size, budget, and staff competencies."[31] When the courts began holding agencies accountable for producing only an EIS document and not necessarily upholding Title I goals, the act was further marginalized by agencies whose missions conflicted with and even contradicted the purpose of NEPA.

NEPA was intended to make federal agencies incorporate environmental considerations into their planning. It is ironic that, if Title I were completely internalized by agencies from day one, comprehensive environmental quality would be a top priority in decision making. This hopeful scenario was a primary reason for creating the EIS. There might be very few extensive EISs deemed necessary if significant impacts were addressed immediately or avoided altogether.

NEPA's Implements of Application: Linking Values and Action with the CEQ and EIS Process

The Council on Environmental Quality's advisory responsibilities are enabled under NEPA. It was created to assist federal agencies with compliance questions and issues, and it is responsible for an annual report advising the president on environmental issues. The CEQ has three major duties: "the analysis and development of national and international environmental policy; the interagency coordination of environmental quality programs; and the acquisition and assessment of environmental data."[1]

The Council on Environmental Quality

The CEQ is a permanent federal agency mandated by NEPA and housed in the executive office of the president. NEPA created a council with three members, appointed by the president and confirmed by the Senate. The president also nominates one member as the chair and the recent precedent has the CEQ as a "council of one."

Section 202 of NEPA created the CEQ not as a regulatory punitive agency such as the Environmental Protection Agency (EPA), but rather as an advisory council that would guide agencies in the NEPA law and provide research on the state of the environment. The CEQ does, however, have the power to issue legally-enforceable regulations regarding the implementation of the EIS process.[2] In *Seattle Community Council Federation v. FAA*, the Ninth Circuit Court described the importance and significance of the CEQ:

> "The regulations promulgated by the Council on Environmental Quality implement the directives and purpose of NEPA. The provisions of [NEPA] and these regulations must be read together as a whole in order to comply with the spirit and letter of the law. The regulations have been enacted in such a way as to remove from the ambit of judicial review any agency decision which meets the requirements of the regulations."[3]

In 1969 President Nixon delegated a task force to study environmental policy, headed by the president of the Conservation Foundation, Russell Train, who later became Nixon's Undersecretary of the Interior. The task force recommended the creation of an interagency, cabinet-level council on the environment. President Nixon therefore opposed locating the CEQ in the executive office of the president, preferring instead a cabinet-level council. But Nixon lost that debate and in good faith appointed council members who understood and supported the act. Russell Train himself became the first chair of the CEQ and played an active role in shaping and implementing environmental policy in the early 1970s.

In 1977, President Jimmy Carter ordered the CEQ to make its 1973 EIS guidelines into formal regulations for agencies to follow during the EIS/NEPA implementation. Subsequently, in 1978 as a part of its role in overseeing NEPA implementation, the CEQ promulgated NEPA regulations and guidelines for federal agencies. In section 1502.1 of those regulations, the CEQ explained the purpose and intent of the impact statement. Rather than having another piece of paperwork for agencies to fill out before their final course of action, CEQ contended that the purpose of the impact statement "is to serve as an action-forcing device to insure that the policies and goals defined in the Act are infused into the ongoing programs and actions of the Federal Government."[4]

Another function of the CEQ, as promulgated in section 309 of the Clean Air Act, requires the agency to review EISs deemed unsatisfactory by the Environmental Protection Agency. Under section 102(2)(c) of NEPA, other federal agencies can challenge the lead agency's proposed action and initiate a CEQ review and recommendation on the disputed impact statement. The CEQ then has sixty days in which to respond. In this time frame, public hearings, mediation sessions, and a scientific environmental review are all slated to occur. Unless the president or senior staff challenges the lead agency's EIS, the most likely avenue for further challenges is the courts.

According to the CEQ's own publication, specific functions of CEQ include the following:

> Advise and assist the President in the development of environmental policies and proposed legislation as requested by the President;
>
> Advise the President on national and international policies relating to the environment;
>
> Identify, assess, and report on trends in environmental quality and recommend appropriate response strategies;
>
> Oversee federal agency implementation of the environmental impact assessment process and act as a referee for interagency disputes regarding the adequacy of such assessments;
>
> Report annually to the President on the state of the environment through preparation of the annual Environmental Quality Report;
>
> Provide general support and leadership to the coordination of activities of the federal departments and agencies which affect, protect, and improve environmental quality;
>
> Support and participate in the government-wide effort to reinvent environmental regulation;
>
> Foster cooperation between the federal, state, and local governments, the private sector, and American citizens on matters of environmental concern;
>
> Interpret NEPA and the CEQ regulations in response to requests from federal, state and local agencies and citizens, and;
>
> Approve agency NEPA procedures and issue guidance to address systemic problems.[5]

Writing the EIS

The elements to be included in the EIS vary from situation to situation and are determined through the scoping process, which as the name suggests, determines the scope of an EIS. The lead agency preparing an EIS is responsible for identifying interested members of the public (local citizens, environmental groups, and businesses) and the other agencies (federal, state, tribal, or local) that may have an interest or stake in the project under consideration. Notices describing the proposed action and requesting input by a certain date are mailed, posted, published, or sometimes disseminated by all three methods. Since the discovery process is designed to determine what should be in an EIS, fundamental questions include a project's significant environmental impacts; the geographic or physical parameters of the study areas; possible alternatives to the proposed action; and any other activity or actions in the study area or any other relevant factors that might have an impact on the project.

The components of a completed EIS depend significantly on the nature of the proposed project. Clearly a project located on a shoreline, for example, would entail considerations different from those of a project located in an urban area. A well-known source book used by environmental professionals for EIS preparation divides the components of an EIS into two categories: the natural environment and the built environment. (See table 5.1 for contrasts between these environments.)

TABLE 5.1

Contrasting Aspects of Natural and Built Environments

Natural Environment	Built Environment
Earth	Land and shoreline use
Geology	Agricultural land, silviculture,
Topography	aquatic mining and other
Unique physical features	extraction activities
Soils	Relationship to existing landuse plans
Erosion	
Habitats for plants and animals	
	Buildings
Water	
Groundwater movement:	**Public Services and Utilities**
quantity/quality	Fire, police, schools, parks or
Surface water improvement:	recreational facilities,
quantity/quality	maintenance, communications,
Public water sources	heat, electrical and water

Runoff/absorption
Floods

supplies, storm removal,
sewage, solid waste disposal

Plants
Number and diversity of
  species
Unique or sensitive
  (threatened or
  endangered) species

Animals (including fish)
Number and diversity of
  species
Fish and wildlife migration
  routes
Unique or sensitive
  (threatened or
  endangered) species

Air
Air quality
Odor

Energy and Other Natural Resources
Amount required, rate and
  efficiency of use
Source/availability
Nonrenewable resources
Conservation and renewable
  resources

Scenic Resources

Transportation
Transportation systems
Vehicular traffic:
  waterborne, rail and air
Movement/circulation of people
  or goods
Traffic hazards
Parking

Environmental Health
Risk of explosion
Releases or potential releases
  to the environment affecting
  public health, such as toxic
  or hazardous materials

Light and Glare

Aesthetics

Recreation

Historic and Cultural Preservation

Source: Adapted from Diori L. Kreske, *Environmental Impact Statements: A Practical Guide for Agencies, Citizens, and Consultants* (New York: John Wiley and Sons, 1996), 281.

Not all items have to be addressed in the EIS. To the list could be added several caveats and qualifications. For example, the courts have made it clear that agencies need to proceed with the EIS process even when they lack complete information necessary to fully assess the impacts of a project. In addition, environmental impact statements need to include the direct effects of a proposed action, but a more significant (and problematic requirement) is that the EIS should also contain indirect impacts that are reasonably foreseeable.[6] There are limits, however. While an agency is required to include in the EIS any information necessary for a reasoned decision, it is not required to obtain that information at exorbitant cost.[7] If it is determined that some data are too costly or difficult to obtain, the EIS must at least indicate what is missing and evaluate its relevance to any reasonable foreseeable adverse impacts.

Such are the technical characteristics of an EIS. These considerations, well known to people in and out of government who prepare EISs, will satisfy the procedural requirements of NEPA. But depending upon how the EIS is prepared, they may, and often do, lack any substantive force. The implementation of the policy, principles, and values of any congressional act is as important as following to the letter any given set of procedural requirements it may contain. NEPA's implementation record has been mixed on this account.

Implementing the EIS Provisions of NEPA: Questions for Federal Agencies

NEPA required formal procedural changes within federal agencies. Federal agencies found that they were faced with a great deal of uncertainty and many unanswered questions. Six issues were especially important:

> When is an EIS necessary?
> Finding that an EIS is necessary, who should prepare it?
> What should be the impact statement's scope and what should it
>   contain?
> At what point should an impact statement be prepared?
> How should an EIS be reviewed?
> How should an EIS utilize public participation?

When is an EIS necessary?

Section 102 has an expansive range of application to agencies and activities. In its Senate Report, Senator Jackson's Interior and Insular Affairs Committee explained NEPA's mandate: "S. 1075, as reported by the committee, would provide all agencies and all federal officials with a legislative mandate and a responsibility to consider the consequences of their actions on the environment. This would be true of the licensing functions of independent agencies as well as the ongoing activities of the regular agencies."[8]

Also included under NEPA's mandate are quasi-judicial independent regulatory commissions. During the Senate hearings, Senator Jackson explained that one of the reasons behind a congressional declaration of environmental policy was the need to modify the mandates of quasi-judicial independent agencies.[9] Pursuant to Executive Order No. 11514, NEPA is applicable to all agency decisions that have an environmental impact, including loans, contracts, leases, licenses, and permits.[10]

About four hundred to five hundred draft and final EISs and an estimated fifty thousand environmental assessments (EAs) were prepared annually in the late 1990s.[11] As the costs (and paper) involved with each EIS have risen over the years, the number of EISs has been greatly reduced, from an annual average of eighteen hundred in the early 1970s.[12]

Generally speaking, an EIS prepared under NEPA will contain the following:

1. Cover Sheet.

2. Executive summary, to describe in sufficient detail (10–15 pages) the critical factors of the EIS so that the reader can become familiar with the proposed project or action and its net effects, the alternatives, and major conclusions.

3. Table of contents.

4. Purpose and need for the action.

5. Alternatives considered by the applicant (proponent), including the do-nothing alternative. The applicant's preferred alternative shall be identified. There must be a balanced description of each alternative.

6. The affected environment. The affected environment on which the evaluation of each alternative was based to include such matters as hydrology, geology, air quality, noise, biology, socioeconomics, energy, land use, archaeology, and history. The total impacts of each alternative must be presented for easy comparison.

7. Coordination. Full consideration must be given to the objectives and suggestions made by local, state, and federal agencies,

and by individual citizens and interest groups. The results of public participation through public meetings or scoping meetings are also included. A list of persons, agencies, and organizations to whom copies of the EIS have been sent shall be included.

8. List of EIS private and public writers and consultants and their qualifications. Persons responsible for a particular analysis shall be identified.

9. Index, commensurate with the complexity of the EIS.

10. Appendices.

11. Material incorporated into an EIS by reference shall be included in a supplemental information document, available for review on request.

12. The format used for EISs shall encourage good analysis and clear presentation of alternatives, including the proposed action and its environmental, economic, and social impacts.

13. The text of a final EIS shall normally be less than 150 pages, and for proposals of unusual scope or complexity shall normally be less than 300 pages.

14. EISs shall be written in plain language with readily understood graphics.[13]

Although NEPA is specifically written for the federal government, very often federal projects involve players from state and local governments and from the private sector. For example, private logging or mining on federal land should require an EIS because the activity is carried out under federal law. Also, federal permits and grants often "federalize" a private or state enterprise, thereby subjecting the proposed project to the EIS process. If a private developer wanted to build a ski resort within a U.S. national forest, he or she would be required to obtain the approval of the Forest Service and would most likely be required to follow NEPA procedures. In fact, NEPA now requires the Department of Agriculture to evaluate the environmental impact of agricultural projects, thus complicating a previously cozy relationship.

Federal agencies have three standard operating procedures for classifying NEPA-related actions: actions that automatically require an EIS; actions with no significant effects and others that may be "categorically excluded" from NEPA compliance; and actions for which the determination of EIS applicability is made with respect to each individual case. According to NEPA, an EIS is required when a federal action is "major" and potentially has a "significant environmental impact." The case law is fairly straightforward: The question of when an environmental impact statement is required has revolved around the definition of "major federal action." The courts have employed a variety of measures to what constitutes a major federal action, including the amount of money to be spent on the proposed project, the geographical space demanded from the project, and whether the project's environmental impacts are long term or short term. Depending on the facts of each case, the court invokes a different set of parameters. An action may be something other than a federally financed construction project; for example, transportation of hazardous materials, a rule change pursuant to the Administrative Procedures Act, proposed congressional legislation and permits issued by federal agencies may also qualify as "major federal actions."

Regulations developed by the Council on Environmental Quality have articulated what "significantly affecting the human environment" means in terms of both intensity and scope. Under NEPA, "impacts," synonymous with "effects," may be either beneficial or harmful. The CEQ's language for implementing NEPA states that impacts include effects on public health or safety, ecologically critical areas, historic sites, and the precedent for future actions.[14] Indirect effects taking place beyond the immediate vicinity or later in time (cumulative impacts) also must be researched and included under NEPA's "significant impact."

> The CEQ's regulations defining "human environment" state that this shall be interpreted comprehensively to include the natural and physical environment and the relationship of people with that environment. This means that economic or social effects are not intended by themselves to require preparation of an environmental impact statement. When an [EIS] is prepared and economic or social and natural or physical environmental effects are interrelated, then the [EIS] will discuss all of these effects on the human environment.[15]

Today, the magnitude of environmental effects is determined by CEQ regulations that characterize "context" and "intensity."[16] Particular attention is paid to direct and indirect effects on the landscape, public health, historic and cultural artifacts, and geographic resources and characteristics. According to NEPA, "the environment" is a very inclusive concept that requires the public in all locations to be provided "safe, healthful, productive, and esthetically and culturally pleasing surroundings."[17] The importance of the substantive mandates for comprehensive environmental analysis are discussed in the next section where we examine the scope of what is to be included in an EIS. Broad scoping ranges for an EIS are important for adequately addressing the human environment.

The environmental assessment process mandated by the National Environmental Policy Act involves several steps. Agency decisions not having a major effect on the environment are exempt from the EIS requirement. The CEQ defines "categorical exclusions" as a category of actions that do not individually or cumulatively have a significant impact on the environment.[18] Some federal actions from the start are clearly seen by all involved as "major" and having a significant effect on the environment.

But while some projects clearly require an EIS, some may go either way. The Environmental Assessment process is a critical juncture for agencies and their corporate partners who would like to avoid the sometimes long and more costly EIS requirement. The EA is required for most agency proposals to determine whether preparation of an EIS is necessary. There are essentially two possibilities from the EA: If no significant impact is found, then the agency makes a "finding of no significant impact" (FONSI), and the project continues; if the project does have a significant impact, it requires an EIS. Agencies may forgo an EA if an EIS is unquestionably necessary or if, on the other hand, the project in question is a "categorical exclusion." Agencies are allowed a considerable degree of discretion when deciding whether they need to prepare an EIS. Of course, if they misuse that discretion, the courts may be used to force agency action. Often an EIS is avoided through the EA finding no significant impact.

In administrative law generally and environmental administrative law in particular, federal courts are likely to give agencies broad latitude when deciding on technical matters (in contrast to procedural matters over which the court is likely to engage in a much stricter review). In the realm of environmental assessments, this judicial attitude has meant that courts have typically given agencies a great deal of discretion in deciding what level of review, an environmental assessment or an environmental impact statement, should have been carried out. In addition, the courts will take into consideration the nature of the impact being examined. For example, courts are likely to give an agency more leeway in matters over which they are routinely involved, such as the U.S. Army Corps of Engineers when it is assessing a dredging permit.

Following the lead of the United States, virtually every developed country and most of the rest of the world have some type of environmental impact statement process. Canada adopted an EA process in 1979 by establishing the Federal Environmental Assessment and Review Process, and the European Community (EC) approved the Environmental Impact Assessment Directive (council directive 85/337) in 1985. The Canadian environmental assessment process is similar to the EIS process in the United States in a number of significant ways. For example, in Canada, as in the United States, an environmental assessment is necessary whenever there is a federal action or an action taken pursuant to federal authority (such as when a permit or a license is required from the federal agency). On the other hand, the European Community directive calls for an assessment regardless of whether the proposed action is undertaken by a private or public entity.

Finding that an EIS is necessary, who should prepare it?

The EIS mechanism has been emulated by many other countries. The lead federal agency—the one leading or funding the proposed project—must file a "notice of intent" in the *Federal Register,* which includes the proposed action, possible alternatives, proposed scoping process, and planned meetings. An EIS prepared in the United States, in contrast to those prepared in Canada or pursuant to directives of the European Community, is prepared by the federal agency or group of agencies involved in the proposed project (or their designees). Some scholars have argued that this is a particular strength of the system in the United States when compared to environmental assessment processes in other countries. Scoping by the lead agency determines the span of issues related to the proposed action to be covered by the EIS. The scope of the EIS helps to determine the EIS agenda, including possible alternative policies' formulation. Hence, U.S. agency procedures (when not Council on Environmental Quality regulations or court precedents) govern the method of determining the choice and evaluating alternatives to a proposed project.

In Canada and the European Community the proponent of a private project is solely responsible for the development of the environmental assessment. (A further weakness of the European Community model is that specific implementation requirements must be passed by member countries. Not all EC members have passed the necessary follow-through legislation.) Private proponents not only submit their proposed development but also develop the environmental assessment document themselves, with no legal requirement that there be any objective evaluation or scrutiny of the alternatives presented in the proposal. This has led one legal scholar to note: "Thus, in Canada and the EC, where there is no objective scrutiny of alternatives as a strict legal requirement, one does not expect to find a thorough analysis of proposals. Alternatives will not be scrutinized and balanced, because to do so requires more time and greater cost. . . . The result, unfortunately, is that the project which is built is not always the best environmental and economic choice."[19]

But even in the United States, scholars of public administration in general and of U.S. environmental administration in particular have long noted that federal agencies that deal with environmental matters tend to bring their own unique perspectives to environmental management problems. Traditionally, for example, the U.S. Army Corps of Engineers has been criticized for having a "build and dam" mentality. Public works engineers, who have a rich tradition of pouring concrete, are likely to see water management as problems to be dealt with by constructing dams and water diversion projects. Although the Corps of Engineers' orientation has changed somewhat since the 1970s, most federal agencies have a particular culture that colors their orientation toward their mission and how they perceive their job. The U.S. Forest Service, to provide another example, has traditionally been oriented more toward timber production and less toward recreation, particularly where it involves wilderness preservation. Under these circumstances we might expect that some federal agencies, on occasion, take a particular slant in the development of an environmental impact statement on a project.

Who's Minding the Store? A Case Study

The Utah Department of Transportation, the state agency whose primary responsibility it is to build and maintain highways, was responsible for writing the environmental impact study for the proposed Legacy Highway, a four-lane alternative to Interstate 15 in southern Davis County.[20] This $284-million highway would, among other things, destroy 160 acres of wetlands and generate a great deal of subsidiary auto-dependent economic activity over its route. The Utah Department of Transportation and opponents of the Legacy Highway (which included among others the Sierra Club, duck hunters with the Farmington Bay Advocates, a group called the Future Moves Coalition, and a transit advocacy organization) disagreed over the adequacy of the draft environmental impact statement proposed for the highway. The highway's opponents were united and vocal in their opinion that the EIS was inadequate. Legacy Highway's opponents argued principally that the Utah Department of Transportation's study virtually ignored the two most important alternatives to constructing the highway—the widening of Interstate 15 or the construction of a commuter rail line. The Utah Department of Transportation's environmental impact statement mentioned and then dismissed the two alternatives as being inadequate to handle traffic projections in twenty years. Critics argued that transportation planners with the State of Utah were too wrapped up in current attitudes about transportation, principally automobile-based, and current trends in land development, with which the Utah Department of Transportation is closely associated. It may only be coincidental that an agency whose training, tradition, and political support has been built on road construction is charged with downplaying or ignoring alternatives to such a traditional means of transportation. The Department of Transportation argued that the three-volume study it produced was "by the book."

The courts were to comment on the final adequacy of this particular EIS, probably sometime in the year 2000. Whatever the outcome of the Legacy Highway issue, clearly we are advantaged in the United States, when compared to European Community countries and Canada, in that our EIS process is at least nominally conducted by public agencies. We also benefit by access to a judicial system that can serve as a check on abuses of agency discretion.

What should be the impact statement's scope and what should it contain?

Section 102(2)(c) of NEPA identifies the five parts that must be included in every environmental impact statement:

1. the environmental impact of the proposed action,
2. any adverse environmental effects that cannot be avoided should the proposal be implemented,
3. alternatives to the proposed action,
4. the relationship between local short-term uses of the environment and the maintenance and enhancement of its long-term productivity, and
5. any irreversible and irretrievable commitments of resources that would be involved in the proposed action should it be implemented.

After an affirmative environmental assessment is issued, the first step in the EIS process is scoping. Scoping is a process that determines the framework of issues and alternatives to be considered in the EIS for the proposed "major federal action." The scope of the proposal determines the extent of alternatives and consequences that will be discussed in the EIS.[21]

Under "scoping" the 1977 CEQ regulations require agencies to consider at least three types of actions, three types of alternatives, and three types of impacts. The actions may be connected, cumulative, and similar actions. The alternatives to such actions must include taking no action, "other reasonable courses of actions," and mitigation measures. Impacts to be discussed must include direct, indirect, and cumulative effects.[22] When an EIS is prepared, it must take into consideration the environmental impacts of the total project, not just one particular component.

The substantive requirements mandated by NEPA are rooted in its legislative history. As the Senate deliberated on NEPA, Senator Jackson argued that the substantive duty of agencies was not only to consider environmental consequences procedurally but also to err on the side of environmental quality and protection when there was a conflict over this in agency decision making. NEPA was originally also intended to combat fragmented federal planning and its environmental consequences. NEPA statutory language and the 1978 CEQ regulations attempt to cut down on the occurrence of such procedures through an interdisciplinary and multiparty scoping process and specific scoping requirements.

NEPA's section 102(2)(a) declares that all federal agencies must "utilize a systematic, interdisciplinary approach which will insure the integrated use of the natural and social sciences and the environmental design arts in planning and in decision making which may have an impact on man's environment." By incorporating many different agencies and other participants into the decision-making process, the authors of NEPA hoped to ensure that the EIS process would reflect a broad scope and specifically include careful ecological analysis.

Yet this means that environmental policy making, indeed the policy-making process in general, in the United States is quite decentralized. In fact, within government at all levels, decision making is often divided up between committees, commissions, boards, and various executive offices. Furthermore, although this book focuses on the federal role in environmental policy, many of the most important environmental decisions are made at the state and local level. This is true in large part because many federal environmental policies provide guidelines but leave implementation up to state and local governments. Those who argue for decreased federal control in environmental or any other policy area often make the case that local governments are in a better position to understand local problems and to fashion local solutions to deal with those problems. For example, the Clean Air Act and the Clean Water Act establish federal environmental regulatory standards that are to be enforced by state and local governments. Critics of this type of decentralization point out that local control can lead to uneven or unequal enforcement of environmental regulations on the local level, as when, for example, a local industry that is economically and politically powerful uses that power to influence local political and regulatory decision making. Critics also point out that the reason for federal standards is to take into consideration broader, more areawide, if not national, concerns. When a pollution problem is regional, along the Mississippi River, for example, only a coordinated management effort will produce policies that benefit all the participants. Yet states on the upper Mississippi have different water quality concerns than do states on the lower Mississippi.

An environmental regulatory problem related to decentralization concerns the organization of environmental programs. The U.S. Environmental Protection Agency is basically organized around specific programs over which Congress has given it enforcement authority. Administrative units within the EPA have substantive policy responsibility for water, solid waste, air and radiation, pesticides, and toxic substances, among others. As rational as this organization may seem from a bureaucratic and political perspective, nature does not always recognize these neat divisions. This type of organization can and often does ignore the interrelationship of environmental problems. Ignoring these interrelationships can lead to situations where the pollutant is pulled out of one medium, such as the land at a toxic waste site, and released into another medium, perhaps as hazardous fumes from a toxic incinerator or as unanticipated runoff. The following case study illustrates the importance and pitfalls of interdisciplinary and multiagency analysis.

Bringing It All Together: The Case of the Portsmouth, Virginia, Oil Refinery

The situation surrounding the location of an oil refinery in Portsmouth, Virginia, illustrates both the problems associated with environmental regulatory decentralization and the "individual medium" approach of environmental laws and policy in the United States.[23]

In 1974 the Hampton Roads Energy Company, 80 percent of which was owned by Cox Enterprises, a large diversified communications corporation, proposed constructing an oil refinery and marine terminal on 623 acres of industrially zoned land on the Elizabeth River in Portsmouth. The Portsmouth refinery would have a capacity of 175,000 barrels of oil a day, and the adjacent marine terminal would be capable of handling a single 285,000-ton tanker or four barges at a time. In addition, storage capacity for 12 million barrels of crude oil would be available. The facility was designed to take heavy, sour crude oil, imported from the Middle East, and desulfurize it to produce light petroleum products such as gasoline and jet fuel. At various stages during the permit process the refinery's proponents argued that U.S. national security would benefit by having the Hampton Roads refinery on the East Coast, eliminating the necessity of importing refined products from refineries in the Caribbean and the Middle East.

Criticisms centered around threats to Virginia's oyster beds, local air quality, and Chesapeake Bay recreation. Most of the oysters harvested in Virginia depend upon seed oysters that originate in the James River. The James River flows into the Elizabeth River, whose valuable oyster seed beds, regarded as irreplaceable, could be damaged from wastewater discharges from the refinery or oil that might wash upstream from tidal flows. Opponents of the refinery included a wide variety of business owners, citizens groups, and governmental units. Opposition to the refinery was organized in a number of different ways. A group of citizens initially organized themselves as the Tidewater Refineries Opposition Fund, later succeeded by Citizens against Refineries' Effects. Opposition also came from seafood trade associations, various civic associations, a number of local and national environmental organizations, and some local medical societies. The refinery was also opposed by the Virginia Institute of Marine Sciences, the Bureau of Shellfish Sanitation in the Virginia Department of Health, the U.S. Fish and Wildlife Service within the U.S. Department of the Interior, and the National Marine Fisheries Service in the U.S. Department of Commerce's National Oceanic and Atmospheric Administration.

The refinery faced a number of formal procedural hurdles. Since the refinery would require the dredging of state-owned bottomland in the Elizabeth River, a "subaqueous permit" was required from the Virginia Marine Resources Commission. The Virginia State Water Control Board, according to the federal Water Pollution Control Act, had responsibility for issuing a "401 certificate" establishing that the dredging and construction necessary for the marine terminal would not violate federal water quality standards or Virginia water quality laws. The Virginia State Water Control Board was also responsible for issuing an "NPDES permit," to allow, also pursuant to the federal Water Pollution Control Act, wastewater to be discharged by the refinery into navigable waters of the United States. The Virginia State Air Pollution Control Board had to issue a permit for air quality pursuant to the requirements of the federal Clean Air Act. The refinery would be a major new source of oxidants in the region, a region that already exceeded federal standards for oxidants. In addition, the federal EPA was responsible for issuing a "prevention of significant deterioration [PSD] permit," again following the Clean Air Act. The PSD permit was necessary for release of pollutants not to exceed federal standards for the region but nonetheless contributing to the overall level of air pollutants within the region. Finally, a "dredge and fill permit" was necessary from the U.S. Army Corps of Engineers, required by the Rivers and Harbors Act of 1899 and the federal Water Pollution Control Act when construction is proposed in U.S. navigable waters.

According to Richard Liroff, who published an extensive study of the Hampton Roads refinery controversy, in all these permitting processes, in addition to numerous local hearings, "No two agencies examined the same

factors in reviewing the environmental impact of the HREC facility."
Some, for example, weighed the importance of national security as a
benefit while others ignored national security questions entirely. Others
evaluated the environmental impacts of their area of responsibility, such
as air, water, or dredging, using widely varying estimations of the potential for or consequences of an oil spill. The only agency and document
that provided an overview of the environmental impacts of the Hampton Roads refinery was the environmental impact statement produced
by the Corps of Engineers.

Proceeding logically and rationally from their view of their legal responsibility, the state and federal regulators involved issued their permits
with or without pertinent oil spill information, wastewater discharge data,
the utility of the existing as opposed to alternative sites, or the overall need
for the project. Ironically, although the Corps of Engineers' EIS provided
the best overview of the environmental impacts of the oil refinery, it did
not, in its initial draft or final environmental impact statements, discuss
the alternatives adequately; hence the corps had to issue additional draft
and final supplemental environmental impact statements. This supplemental EIS was eventually held inadequate by a district court, and the
proponent abandoned the project after eight years (due in part to a down-
turn in the oil market).

In the decentralized context of U.S. environmental policy and regulation, both in terms of regulatory authority and in terms of the focus of
regulation, an EIS may, as in the case of the Hampton Roads refinery, provide a much-needed overview of environmental impacts. However, as this
case study also illustrates, agencies may use the EIS procedure to suit their
own ends, thereby setting up a contentious context for EIS implementation
and interpretation. For example, in 1973 an Atomic Energy Commission's
EIS for a single breeder reactor was found by the Second Federal District
Court to be inadequate. The federal court held that the EIS must cover the
entire breeder reactor program. The *Scientists' Institute for Public Information* court decision held that NEPA required agencies to study all plausible
impacts, including cumulative effects on the environment that may result
from multiple sources over time.[24]

Yet to avoid addressing the cumulative and synergistic effects of a
project, federal agencies can push for a narrow or fragmented EIS scope.
For example, say, the Bureau of Reclamation wants to build a series of ten

dams along a river. Because the individual environmental consequences for each dam appear to have less of an impact on the environment than would appear on a cumulative analysis, the Bureau of Reclamation could try to effectively evade NEPA by having ten individual impact statements. This segmented scope would effectively ignore the larger ecosystem requirements and the overall environmental costs of all the dam-building projects taken together.

Studying cumulative effects is critical for environmental quality. In a 1997 Council on Environmental Quality handbook, "Considering Cumulative Effects under the National Environmental Policy Act," the CEQ states that "while it is difficult to predict and assess even direct effects with a high degree of certainty, learning to assess cumulative effects is essential to sustainable development."[25] According to the 1978 CEQ regulations, "'Cumulative impact' is the impact on the environment which results from the incremental impact of the action when added to other past, present, and reasonably foreseeable future actions regardless of what agency (federal or nonfederal) or person undertakes such other actions. Cumulative impacts can result from individually minor but collectively significant actions taking place over a period of time."[26] In 1997, the Ninth Circuit Court of Appeals reaffirmed the importance of cumulative impact analysis by ordering the Federal Highway Administration and the California Department of Transportation to take a harder look at the cumulative impact of a new road proposal.[27]

Although NEPA emphasized a comprehensive analysis of all relevant program proposals, the courts have consistently used the "rule of reason" and the standards against "arbitrary and capricious decisions" under the Administrative Procedure Act.[28] Through judicial review the EIS's substantive policy objectives for ensuring a healthy environment have been scaled down considerably. An agency needs to consider how to mitigate environmental impacts but does not have to show it fully complies with Title I of the act. Environmental impact statements in the United States are required, among other things, to examine the alternatives to a proposed project. Failure of the proposing agency to adequately examine the alternatives, as well as failure to undertake additional evaluations, are subject to judicial review. CEQ regulations describe the presentation of alternatives as the "heart" of the procedural process. As the regulations stipulate, NEPA documents must "rigorously explore and objectively evaluate all reasonable alternatives" and "devote substantial treatment to each alternative considered in detail" and discuss why alternatives were eliminated.[29]

Bureaucratic interpretations of "reasonable" alternatives, however, often conflict with environmentalists' wish for paradigmatic changes or citizens' interest in long-term planning. Furthermore, the courts have not specified the types of alternatives to be considered for proposals found deficient. The range of alternatives is also affected by other environmental policies and goals. For example, NEPA does not explicitly explain how to discuss energy alternatives in the absence of a coherent national energy policy. Consequently, the range of energy alternatives at the national level continues to favor dependence on fossil fuels and nuclear power over renewable solar and wind energy sources.

At what point should an impact statement be prepared?

Since preparation of an EA, EIS, or both is usually required with every major federal action significantly affecting the human environment, part 1501 of the CEQ regulations, "NEPA and Agency Planning," states that agencies must integrate "the NEPA process into early planning to insure appropriate consideration of NEPA's policies and to eliminate delay."[30] The CEQ found that the NEPA process is often initiated too late in the planning process to be fully effective.[31]

However, preparing an EA too early may lead to an inaccurate assessment because some information may be unknown, incomplete, or inadequate. At the same time, statements written late in the decision-making process will most likely have less effect because the proposed designs will be nearly complete and the EIS will merely fulfill the bare minimum procedural requirements. On the other hand, by incorporating NEPA's requirements early enough, such as generating project alternatives and involving other agencies and the public, poor projects are more likely to be avoided, and support for the adequately planned project may be increased because in most cases full public participation in planning ensures widespread support for a quality project choice.

The timing conundrum was addressed in a 1973 D.C. Appeals Court case called *Scientist's Institute for Public Information (SIPI) v. Atomic Energy Commission.* In *SIPI* the AEC claimed that, because they were only researching plans for developing a liquid fast-breeder reactor for nuclear power plants, there was no need for an EIS. The AEC acknowledged that construction or operational plans would require an EIS, but they argued that NEPA did not apply to research and development plans. Judge Skelly Wright authored the D.C. Circuit Court's finding that the agency's attempt to dodge NEPA's EIS requirement was an "unnecessarily crabbed approach" to NEPA. Judge Wright concluded that the AEC's plans involved a "major federal action" that would "significantly" affect "the quality of the human environment" and thus required an EIS. The court identified four relevant factors for deciding when to require an EIS: (1) the commercial feasibility of the technology or project in the near future; (2) information available on the effects of implementing the technology; (3) the extent to which the technology involves irretrievable commitments and eliminates alternative options; and (4) the environmental impact of the technology when fully implemented at the commercial level.[32] The CEQ regulations that mandate an impact statement for all qualified proposals reflect the court's approach in *SIPI*. The CEQ defines "proposal" as follows:

> Proposal exists at that stage in the development of an action when an agency subject to the Act has a goal and is actively preparing to make a decision on one or more alternative means of accomplishing that goal, and the effects can be meaningfully evaluated. Preparation of an environmental impact statement on a proposal should be timed (§1502.5) so that the final statement may be completed in time for the statement to be included in any recommendation or report on the proposal. A proposal may exist in fact as well as by agency declaration that one exists.[33]

Based on Judge Wright's four part balancing test, which of course predated the 1978 CEQ regulations, the Court of Appeals ruled that an EIS was necessary. The EIS proceeded to expose "the issues of plutonium radiation hazards and runaway costs, and led to Congress' deauthorization of the reactor."[34]

The EIS process starts at the time a proposal is made for a federal action significantly affecting the environment. In *Aberdeen and Rockfish Railroad Company v. Students Challenging Regulatory Agency Procedures* (1975), the U.S. Supreme Court found that "where an agency initiates federal action by publishing a proposal and then holding hearings on the proposal, the statute would appear to require that an impact statement be included in the proposal and considered at the hearing."[35] According to *Aberdeen* there was a thin line between an early but insufficient EIS, and a late EIS that is a post-hoc justification for the predetermined agency choice. Standards for the EIS process have since been streamlined and the timing of EIS preparation is uniform across federal agencies. But as in the following case study, information in an EIS can be woefully inaccurate.

The Alaskan Oil Pipeline: A Case Study

One of the earliest, and most interesting, EIS experiences involved the trans-Alaska pipeline.[36] The development of the EIS for the trans-Alaska pipeline illustrates some of the problems inherent in EIS preparation, the politics of EIS preparation, and how the procedural niceties can be met, and negative environmental problems identified, addressed, and dismissed.

Oil was discovered in Prudhoe Bay on Alaska's Arctic-Ocean North Shore in 1968. Within months of the discovery of oil, the major petroleum explorers in the region, Atlantic Richfield (now ARCO), Humble Oil (now Exxon-Mobil), and British Petroleum (now BP), decided to build a pipeline to move the oil to market. The oil companies involved in Alaska exploration banded together and created the Alyeska Pipeline Service Company to construct and manage the trans-Alaska pipeline. Alyeska is owned by seven oil companies: BP owns 50 percent, ARCO 21.4 percent, Exxon-Mobil 24.4 percent, Unocal 4.1 percent, Amerada Hess 1.5 percent, and Phillips 1.4 percent. Initially estimated to cost $900 million, the trans-Alaska pipeline ultimately cost $8 billion—the most expensive privately financed construction project in history. Carrying oil from Prudhoe Bay to the port of Valdez, 800 miles away, the pipeline has transported billions of gallons of North Shore crude.

Just three months after President Nixon signed NEPA, necessitating an EIS for the pipeline, the Department of Interior, on March 20, 1970, issued the first pipeline environmental impact statement—perhaps one of the first ever produced in the United States. It was eight pages long. This EIS was quickly challenged, and on April 23, 1970, Federal District Court Judge George Hart found that this initial EIS did not comply with NEPA. Shortly thereafter the Department of the Interior began work on what would become the actual Alaska pipeline EIS. With the Bureau of Land

Management as the lead agency, an interagency federal task force on Alaska oil development was created, chaired by the undersecretary of the interior, and made up of representatives from the Departments of Defense; Transportation; Commerce; Health, Education, and Welfare; Housing and Urban Development; the Office of Science and Technology; Management and Budget; the CEQ; the EPA; and the National Science Foundation. In addition, within the Department of Interior the Bureaus of Indian Affairs, Sports Fisheries and Wildlife, Geological Survey, Office of Oil and Gas, and the Office of the Science Advisor were involved in the preparation of the draft EIS.

The first draft statement was released by the Department of the Interior on January 15, 1971. In December, 1970, the Department sent a copy of its first draft to the Alyeska Pipeline Service Company for its review prior to its release, which resulted in extensive editing. The first draft was issued to a wide range of federal agencies for comment, and public hearings were held in Washington, D.C., in mid-February, 1971, and for nine days in Anchorage, Alaska, at the end of February. Nearly three hundred individuals testified at the hearings, representing a wide range of organizations and generating ten thousand pages of testimony—much of it critical.

Then in March, 1972, the Interior Department released the final EIS, comprising six volumes and three supplemental volumes, which purportedly cost $11 million to produce. On May 4, 1972, the Center for Law and Social Policy in Washington, D.C., representing three environmental organizations, sued in federal court to challenge the issuing of a construction permit for the pipeline and submitted four volumes of criticism of the EIS and the project. The Alaska pipeline EIS contained no original research, relying on data that had been generated by the Alyeska Pipeline Company for all its conclusions, and was full of generalizations about what could happen under certain circumstances—the kind of language that if accurate is also vague and uncertain and has become boilerplate in the writing of an EIS.

The federal courts never specifically addressed the question of the adequacy of the final pipeline EIS. Judicial determination of what would make for an adequate EIS would have to wait for later decisions. The 1973 Arab oil embargo, and the long gas lines that accompanied it, provided the backdrop for the final chapter in the Alaska pipeline EIS saga. In November, 1973, Congress passed the Trans-Alaska Pipeline Authorization Act, which among other things, directed the secretary of the interior to authorize construction of the pipeline and barred courts from considering environmental lawsuits. The Trans-Alaska Pipeline Authorization Act was a very controversial measure. Vice President Spiro T. Agnew had to cast the tie-breaking vote to achieve passage and, during the debate, Secretary of the Interior Rogers Morton publicly promised Congress that Alaskan oil would move in the safest manner possible, including the use of double-hull tankers. The double-hull tanker requirement was later dropped after pressure from the oil companies. (Many people feel that had double-hull tankers been required, the 1989 *Exxon Valdez* oil spill would have been prevented.)

The Alaska pipeline EIS provides interesting examples of how an EIS can address—and dismiss—potential environmental problems. Although the Alaska pipeline EIS never received a final judicial determination of its adequacy, it would appear upon reading that it satisfied the procedural requirements of NEPA—that is, alternatives were identified and the environmental problems associated with the alternatives were laid out.

Of course, hindsight is 20/20. But in light of how the pipeline has been managed and the things that have happened since construction was completed, it is interesting to note what the pipeline EIS did not do. For example, the EIS carefully pointed out that human activities are subject to error and there was no way to know whether there might be a serious oil spill in the pipeline or its transportation systems. Nonetheless it used several models that averaged the amount of losses over time from different types of transportation systems and concluded that about 140,000 gallons of oil could be lost in a year from tanker casualties in its worst-case, or maximum casualty discharge, scenario. In this context it is important to remember that most of the controversy surrounding the construction of the Alaska oil pipeline was not over *whether* a pipeline would be built but rather *what route* the pipeline would take. Most environmental organizations pushed for an overland route transversing Canada to a distribution point somewhere in the upper Midwest. These environmental organizations argued that a pipeline that relied on tanker transport would be, in the words of Brock Evans of the Sierra Club, "an environmental disaster." Consequently projections and estimations of the potential damage from a tanker oil spill were crucial.

It is difficult to imagine that there would not be a major spill connected with the Alaska pipeline sometime in its lifetime. The pipeline, initially designed to function for thirty years, would be hauling roughly 25 percent of U.S. domestic oil consumption. Moving all that oil across eight hundred miles and then into tankers over a thirty-year period would almost certainly result in the likelihood of a major spill. The *Ocean Eagle* oil spill on March 4, 1968, in San Juan, Puerto Rico, dumped 2.85 million gallons of oil into the San Juan area. The South Timbalier oil well spill off Louisiana on December 1, 1970, dumped 2.2 million gallons of oil into the Gulf of Mexico, and there had been other oil spills elsewhere in the world. Yet the EIS compilers projected 140,000 gallons as the worst-case scenario. The *Exxon Valdez* oil spill in Prince William Sound on March 24, 1989, emitted 10.9 million gallons of crude oil into Alaskan waters.

The Alaskan pipeline EIS was also careful to point out that the pipeline would require much higher levels of maintenance and safety than an ordinary pipeline and, due to the fragility of the Alaskan environment, would require careful monitoring. These were clear warnings and guidelines designed for the management of the pipeline. But here the EIS seems to have provided little guidance. In 1993 an audit of the pipeline management commissioned by the Bureau of Land Management found that Alyeska's assurance of quality programs had been "dysfunctional," and furthermore, there were "no reasonable guarantees that the pipeline was even built properly, much less maintained in a way that protects public safety and the environment." The report went on to find that safety surveillance and internal audits had been so lax and superficial that it was difficult to estimate risk involved and that there were "massive violations" of the National Electrical Code, those rules designed to limit the risks of fires and electrocution, creating a serious safety risk along the length of the pipeline. There have been other serious maintenance problems. Since 1977 half a dozen of the fourteen serious pipeline spills—those exceeding the 750-barrels-per-day threshold (31,500 gallons)—should have set off an alarm but the alarm system didn't work. In short, the EIS clearly pointed out how important maintenance of the pipeline would be, but these recommendations were ignored. Should the warnings developed in the EIS process have teeth? Currently they do not.

The pipeline EIS pointed out that "disturbances associated with construction activities and road and pipeline maintenance and operation would have adverse effect on large mammals inhabiting the proposed right-of-way in areas adjacent to the pipeline route." It went on to note that "disturbance to wildlife would disrupt normal behavior patterns, would generate increased physiological stress, and would force less adaptable species from the areas of activity," and that although it was difficult to estimate the exact impact on caribou in the area, "disturbance during and immediately following birth can result in substantial decrease in survival of the newborn young in moose, mountain sheep, and caribou." An EIS has satisfied its statutory requirement if it identifies a potential environmental problem associated with whatever alternatives are being examined. The pipeline EIS identified those problems. In the case of the caribou, the result seems to be less drastic than environmentalists had predicted. In fact, the caribou populations in Prudhoe Bay itself are significantly greater than they were prior to construction. Biologists are quick to point out, however, that this population in fact includes fewer calf-bearing females than were originally in the area and that we do not know what the long-term impacts on caribou populations will be.

The Alaska pipeline EIS provides some interesting examples of what is good and what is less good about the EIS process. Basically the pipeline EIS admitted that much could happen and developed worst-case scenarios, although in the case of oil spills the worst case was not in fact the worst that did happen. The EIS was written in language so vague that it covered almost any uncertainty. In the final volume of the six-volume EIS, many of the concerns raised by individuals at the hearings are stated and either directly addressed or dismissed as unimportant, which has become common practice in EIS preparation. The maintenance and safety recommendations of this EIS, which could have provided valuable guidance for the future, were ignored. The EIS also included recommendations for emergency preparedness in terms of the amount of supplies and materials that would be needed in the event of an oil spill. Unfortunately, these recommendations were based on its own minimal worst-case scenario oil spill and hence, as was learned during the *Exxon Valdez* disaster, were woefully inadequate.

Finally, the Alaska pipeline EIS illustrates the very political nature of the process. When all was said and done, the seeming political expediency of completing the pipeline overrode environmental concerns. Congress basically pulled the pipeline out of the courts to authorize construction. In the end, politics can be paramount.

How should an EIS be reviewed?

NEPA's section 102 mandated an interagency review process that had not previously existed for most federal agencies. Initially, there were five central questions about the review process between U.S. federal agencies. First, which agencies are to review the proposal? Second, at what stage in the project's process are other agencies to comment? Third, are the commenting agencies' reviews to focus on the quality of the EIS writing, the merits and substantive impact of the proposed action, or both? Fourth, are review comments to make normative conclusions as to the EIS decision of the originating agency? Finally, in what way are the lead agencies to respond to the other agencies' comments?

Agencies have had considerable discretion in acting upon these questions.[37] According to CEQ regulations, a "cooperating agency" means any federal agency, other than the lead agency, which has jurisdiction by law or special expertise with respect to any environmental impact involved in a proposal (or a reasonable alternative) for legislation or other major federal action significantly affecting the quality of the human environment. The selection and responsibilities of such a cooperating agency are also described.[38] A state or local agency, others with similar qualifications, or when the effects are on a reservation, an Indian tribe may by agreement with the lead agency become a "cooperating agency." For example, a company proposes to increase gold mining on Forest Service national forest land adjacent to Yellowstone National Park. The rationale behind this project is mainly economic. The company would enlarge its power and resources with another mine, and the local community tax base would increase. The National Park Service (NPS) may be against this proposal but it is beyond its jurisdiction. However, the NPS opinion will be included in both the scoping and commenting stages of the EIS process as a "cooperating agency." But ultimately, the key players will be the Forest Service, the EPA, the president, and if a lawsuit is filed, the federal court system.

Once an agency has reached the stage of preparing a draft environmental impact statement, the Environmental Protection Agency has the option to exercise a prominent role in the NEPA impact statement process. The review of impact documents is the domain of the EPA and organized within the Environmental Review Process and the Federal Facilities Compliance Program. The EPA is authorized to review EIS documents, particularly the draft environmental impact statements, by way of several congressional acts. First, NEPA requires that all federal agencies proposing legislation and other major actions significantly affecting the natural environment consult with other agencies having statutory jurisdiction or special expertise over respective environmental questions. In this consultation process, other agencies, especially the EPA, are granted the opportunity to review and comment on documents generated in the EIS process. Section 309 of the Clean Air Act requires the EPA to review and issue written comments on any matter relating to that act. In addition, section 309 authorizes the EPA to review major federal projects for construction or other actions to which NEPA's section 102(2)(c) applies.

Finally, EPA reviews of other federal agency activity, as stipulated by the Safe Drinking Water Act and the Federal Water Pollution Control Act, are integrated into the Environmental Review Process. According to the EPA, the objective of the Environmental Review Process is to empower the agency to use its unique expertise in environmental issues to ensure that NEPA's goal of environmental quality is met. The EPA's review process is implemented, in conjunction with related EPA duties, to (1) participate in interagency coordination early in the planning process to identify significant environmental issues that should be addressed in completed documents; (2) conduct follow-up coordination on actions where the EPA has identified significant environmental impacts to ensure a full understanding of the issues and to ensure implementation of appropriate corrective actions; and (3) identify environmentally unsatisfactory proposals and consult with other agencies, including the CEQ, to achieve timely resolution of the major issues and problems.[39]

At every EPA regional office several employees are assigned to work on the Environmental Review Process along with staff members at EPA headquarters in Washington, D.C. The review process involves the use of two scales to evaluate draft impact statements. One is a four-point ratings system that evaluates the impact of the proposed action. The review categories, from "no concern" to "great concern" regarding environmental impact of an agency's preferred alternative, range from (1) lack of objections, (2) environmental concerns, (3) environmental objections, and (4) environmentally unsatisfactory. The second scale used by the EPA to review draft environmental impact statements concerns the quality of information in the impact statement. The categories include adequate, insufficient, and inadequate information. Both sets of reviews take place at one of the ten EPA Regional Offices, with minimal input from headquarters in Washington, D.C., unless the evaluation is adjudged unsatisfactory or inadequate by the regional office.

For several reasons, it is reasonable to expect that negative EPA ratings for both impact and information would have declined since the EPA started reviewing draft impact statements. First, since agencies presumably have benefited from prior NEPA implementation and guidance, one might assume that they have learned how to prepare better documents that meet NEPA's procedural and substantive goals. Second, information is now easier to acquire and transmit. Third, every agency that has received negative ratings is required to meet with the EPA to determine how it can improve its NEPA compliance. Fourth, under the leadership of EPA commissioner Carol Browner, appointed by President Clinton in 1992, the EPA expressed a desire to take more of a partnership role in the NEPA process rather than as a final arbiter, so EPA officials can collaborate on the preparation of the document from the early stages of EIS preparation. These four reasons lead one to expect that EPA ratings for NEPA documents would have improved with time.

According to a study of EPA ratings, however, it has become more difficult to receive a top rating from the EPA. On both scales—quality of preferred alternative and quality of information—ratings have shown a "substantial decline" in the number of "good" ratings in both categories. Kelly Tzoumis and Linda Finegold found that the top rating a draft environmental impact statement can receive, "lack of objections" (LO), sharply declined in frequency in 1982 and has since stabilized as an infrequent EPA rating. The authors speculated that the sudden drop in LOs in 1982 was a counterreaction by career civil servants in the regional EPA offices to President Reagan's appointment of Anne Buford, an "anti-environmentalist," as EPA commissioner. The stabilization of low numbers of LOs after 1984 is attributed in part to EPA raters relying more heavily on the new middle-ground category, "environmental concerns," created in 1984.[40]

The study also found that the top rating for quality of information, "adequate," has dropped off since the late 1970s and has consistently occurred with less frequency than the EPA's middle category, "insufficient." According to Tzoumis and Finegold, "The information ratings show that documents are not using the longevity of experience with EIS preparation in a meaningful manner." Another explanation they offered is heightened expectations on the part of EPA raters because information is more readily available than in the past.[41] Clearly the preparation of environmental impact statements leaves much to be desired if judged only on the infrequency of top NEPA ratings offered by the EPA.

How should an EIS utilize public participation?

The framers of NEPA wanted the public not only to be aware of and informed about environmentally damaging federal projects but also to have an active role in commenting on the agency's decisions. The statute and its CEQ implementing regulations operate like other "sunshine" laws (e.g., the Administrative Procedures Act) in that they require full disclosure to the public as well as extensive public hearings and opportunities for comment on the proposed project. These procedures are intended to produce more democratic political decision making.

Since its enactment, NEPA has significantly improved the integration and coordination of public information into agency decision making. According to the CEQ's 1997 "Effectiveness Study," "The success of a NEPA process heavily depends on whether an agency has systematically reached out to those who will be most affected by a proposal, gathered information and ideas from them, and responded to the input by modifying or adding alternatives throughout the entire course of a planning process."[42] Open hearings are specifically required to gather comments of the public regarding the scope of an EIS. NEPA requires the lead agency to provide adequate detail of the environmental consequences. Although the general parameters of NEPA are determined by CEQ regulations, a considerable amount of discretion is granted to the lead agency.

It is not uncommon for controversial EIS documents to be well over 500 pages long and amount to several volumes, even though CEQ guidelines limit typical environmental impact statements to 150 pages or, when necessitated by complexity or unusual scope, 300 pages. In a study done by the EPA in 1996, researchers found that the average length of draft EISs was 198 pages of text and 385 total pages. The shortest EIS was 55 pages and the longest was 1,622 pages of text.[43] Elizabeth Blaug, as an attorney for the CEQ, reported that environmental assessments are also much lengthier than their official 15-page minimum. Many EIS and EA reports can be quite difficult to read—especially for a lay person—as they can be enormous and highly technical, despite section 1502.10 of the 1978 CEQ regulations requiring EIS language to be accessible to the general public. CEQ guidelines specifically direct that environmental impact statements avoid jargon and unnecessarily technical terms. The EIS executive summary is often all that is read by decision makers and many public participants.

Given that most of the affected public are not trained in law, ecology, or public administration, it is critical for agencies to be more creative in their public outreach. The 1997 CEQ study of NEPA found that "creating a true partnership with the community involves more than holding a hearing and making documents available. Public involvement, that's effort—and time."[44] Traditional public hearings can be limited to largely one-way communication that does not respect the ideas and needs of the public; this violates the spirit of NEPA. Because these procedural requirements are legally enforceable, their violation has opened the door to a flood of environmental litigation brought by environmental organizations.

NEPA and International Federal Action

It is clear that environmental issues are becoming increasingly international in scope. Coinciding and related to this, is the globalization of the economy and the increased pressure upon the world's natural resources. The U.S. federal government is obviously a major player in the transformation of the global economy and what happens to the earth as a living ecosystem (the Gaia Theory). How and when should NEPA apply to federal agency decisions and actions that effect non-U.S. territory? Conservative federal courts "have generally held that the activities of federal agencies abroad are not bound by U.S. statutory law except where Congress has specifically imposed conditions (as in the 'Foley Doctrine')."[45] In response to similar issues, President Carter's Executive Order 12114 (1979) defined environmental impact and harm to be based on "its geographical location and not on the location of the action." More recently, the CEQ issued a memo to the heads of agencies regarding NEPA's transboundary effects. In this memo, the CEQ reiterates NEPA's goals of geo-political sustainability and also refers to the case law requiring U.S. EISs to include effects across all affected political borders (e.g. state and national borders). The CEQ suggests that agencies include all foreseeable transboundary effects in the scoping process. According to the CEQ memo, "agencies should be particularly alert to actions that may affect migratory species, air quality, watersheds, and other components of the natural ecosystem that cross borders, as well as to interrelated social and economic effects.[46]

The legislative intent regarding NEPA's application to extraterritorial actions and impacts indicated an awareness of the importance of U.S. agencies' impact and the planetary nature of environmental impacts. A U.S. House of Representatives 1971 report on Administration of the National Environmental Policy Act stated that "the history of the Act makes it quite clear that the global effects of environmental decisions are inevitably a part of the decision-making process and must be considered in that context." As Caldwell notes, "in 1978, testifying in a hearing on a bill to exempt certain activities of the Export-Import Back from NEPA, Senator Edmund Muskie declared that, 'in my view, the intention of the National Environmental Policy Act and the environmental impact statement was to apply to major Federal actions wherever they impact within the United States or outside.' The CEQ has consistently supported this interpretation."[47]

Agencies and Implementation

Several years after NEPA was signed, Richard Liroff assessed the effectiveness of NEPA within federal agencies. Liroff noted:

> Several general patterns of agency response to NEPA are observable. First, there were those agencies with the AEC [the Atomic Energy Commission] prior to *Calvert Cliffs* and the FPC [the Federal Power Commission] who felt that compliance might interfere with their achievements of their traditional missions. Second, there was a lack of procedural response on the part of environmental agencies like [the] EPA that regarded NEPA as superfluous because their decisions were already infused with environmental considerations.[48]

Liroff also notes how a few agencies were forced to comply after strong lower court decisions enforcing NEPA. In addition, Liroff concludes that in many agencies, protecting the environment yields little positive feedback when an agency's mission focuses on other goals. In 1976 Richard N. L. Andrews concluded that

> agencies' responses to NEPA are still evolving, though at a slower rate than in the early years. . . . Generally accepted interpretations have been developed for many of the early questions that arose, and despite important remaining differences, NEPA's procedural requirements have generally been assimilated into agency practice. Yet many lawsuits are still being filed and often won against the agencies, and the threat of controversy continues to exert a pervasive cautionary force on agencies contemplating environmentally significant actions; and as long as this force exists, continued evolution may be expected in agency efforts to cope with it and adapt to it.[49]

The reluctance of the federal bureaucracy to incorporate all of NEPA into its decision-making processes is not surprising. Faced with NEPA's broad policy directives, such as to "fulfill the responsibilities of each generation as trustee of the environment for succeeding generations" and to "assure for all Americans safe, healthful, productive, and aesthetically and culturally pleasing surroundings," agencies were forced to contend with radically new normative demands, whereas NEPA's procedural requirements were seemingly easier to understand and measure. However, a procedure cannot be understood in a vacuum. An EIS produced in a spirit antithetical to the act's moral foundations is contradictory. The procedures required by NEPA and expanded on by the CEQ are based directly on NEPA's substantive considerations. By complying with the EIS process, agencies are forced to answer qualitative and quantitative environmental questions about their proposed decisions. Although investigating the immediate and cumulative effects of an agency's preferred action (and its alternatives) is an important first step in achieving the goals of NEPA's framers, the subsequent agency actions need to reflect NEPA's broad environmental policy vision of sustainability.

The procedural requirements encourage mitigation efforts, as well as public discourse, information, and participation. Before NEPA came into effect, environmental values were rarely represented in agency decision making; so despite congressional recognition of environmental concerns, federal agencies were reluctant to make major changes in their routine decision making. Early lower court decisions about NEPA, like *Calvert Cliffs'*, speeded up NEPA compliance within federal agencies by requiring strict compliance with the act's procedures.[50] Now, nearly thirty years later, the NEPA EIS process is, for better and worse, an industry in itself.

Conclusion

Passage of NEPA was clearly a paradigm shift for federal environmental policy.[51] It was a seminal policy that introduced the federal government to environmental questions comprehensively for the first time. NEPA also injected ecological discipline and principles into agency decision making. Finally, it strengthened the power of Congress in overseeing federal agency actions affecting the natural environment and the general welfare of humanity and afforded citizens the opportunity to participate in federal decision making. NEPA's legislative history and the express language of the statute make it clear that Congress intended for federal agencies to use a comprehensive approach to environmental decision making, incorporating the latest technology and information available, and to base their decisions on environmental values in addition to other interests.

However, even though NEPA actively directs agencies to take into account environmental effects of their actions, this does not guarantee that agencies will do so. Given such a broadly worded statute as NEPA, agency administrators are left with considerable discretion as to precisely how to implement NEPA's goals in their decision making. There is often a considerable gulf between the intentions of NEPA's creators, the environmental decisions of federal agencies, and court rulings on implementation of NEPA's requirements. Even though the act attempts to provide a comprehensive national direction for environmental policy through its purpose and Title I and their basis for the EIS, court interpretations of the statute have varied. Judicial decisions often held federal agencies responsible only for producing an environmental impact statement as set forth in section 102, and did not review the final outcome or decision of the agency. Thus NEPA is subject to administrative and judicial interpretations that often significantly diminish the act's overall effectiveness within the federal bureaucracy.

Dinah Bear, former general counsel at the CEQ, wrote that "because NEPA is most often considered a procedural statute, there is a tendency to elevate perfection of process over common sense and substance."[52] When the importance of fulfilling procedures outweighs the duty to achieve NEPA's environmental policies, Robert Davis suggests it is akin to "watching someone smoke himself to death, content in the knowledge that the cigarette package contains a warning about the dangers of smoking."[53] Unless agency bureaucrats, presidents, Congress, and the courts begin to see NEPA as a tool for quality decision making to foster collaboration among disparate interest groups and to ensure environmental quality, NEPA will merely ensure that "irresponsible environmental damage was conducted intentionally" with public participation.[54] Remembering NEPA's founding and history is especially important, as NEPA's implementation is often something less than what NEPA's founders expected.

CHAPTER 6

The Courts and Environmental Policy:
NEPA's Judicial Downsizing

NEPA's effect on the administrative state, on the management, procedures, and processes employed in the bureaucracy, is profound. But the place for resolving U.S. differences and environmental conflicts over values is not only in the halls of Congress. The courts are also centers of environmental policy disputes. This is particularly true for interest groups lacking the power and access necessary to influence lawmakers in more traditional political arenas such as Congress or state legislatures. In addition, many environmental law firms and organizations maintain themselves on the financial settlements of their cases, creating a strong incentive for them to pursue environmental litigation. This chapter reviews NEPA's evolution within the courts. Despite NEPA's brevity and lack of any judicial review language in the statute itself, the statute has resulted in more than one thousand court cases.[1] Following the courts' views and interpretations of NEPA "not only clarifies the law of NEPA but also illustrates the process by which courts shape the flight of the statutory 'missile' after the legislature launches it."[2]

The judicial branch of government plays a crucial role in NEPA's effectiveness. The courts are often the final check on whether or not NEPA is properly implemented by the executive branch. Relief under NEPA, however, is not intended to be punishment, only remedial. Thus, parties cannot sue, say, the Department of Defense to "teach them a lesson," only to "fix" a specific current issue. The courts' role is limited and shaped by the precedents and standards by which U.S. federal courts operate.

When examining the judicial history of NEPA interpretations it is important to keep in mind major factors influencing the nature of administrative law and judicial review in the United States. Above all, for a variety of reasons, U.S. courts are more comfortable deciding cases on the basis of law rather than on disputed fact. Laws can be read and understood by judges trained in law. The facts of an environmental case, on the other hand, usually deal with scientific and technical matters with which judges are not familiar. The courts generally try to stay out of controversies concerning the way an agency has gone about performing regulatory analysis.

Thus when there are technical considerations in dispute, courts are likely to defer to agency discretion. And courts give agencies wide discretion in interpreting regulations that are ambiguous and unclear. As the Supreme Court ruled in *Chevron, U.S.A. v. Natural Resources Defense Council:* "If the statute is silent or ambiguous with respect to the specific issue, the question for the court is whether the agency's answer is based on a permissible construction of the statute."[3] Generally, the courts will question an agency's interpretation of a regulation only if they find that the agency's action was "arbitrary and capricious." Deference to agency decisions in preference to dealing with questions of law has operated to produce a judicial environment not conducive to an ecological reading of NEPA's substantive policy language.

In some cases, court injunctions and decisions have stopped environmentally deleterious projects and impacts. However, nearly all litigation is focused on an agency's failure to meet NEPA procedural requirements rather than on meeting its substantive goals of sustainability and a "harmonious" relationship between humans and the natural environment. The courts have consistently and rigorously interpreted NEPA's procedural requirements—the EIS—while ignoring or dismissing any requirement that agencies alter decisions having an adverse environmental impact.

This chapter pays closest attention to questions of legal standing, standards of review, scope of NEPA's judicial inquiry, and content of policies and action. These four variables are particularly important because each shows how the courts have whittled away at NEPA's administrative muscle and fundamental purpose of protecting the environment by preventing environmentally harmful projects.

Law and the Environment

A number of long-standing judicial remedies in common law deal with pollution and environmental damage. In environmental litigation, particularly by plaintiffs seeking to prevent pollution or some other undesired activity, the "public nuisance" doctrine has historically been employed. Since NEPA's inception in 1970, however, the most common legal challenge by environmentalist plaintiffs is to enforce NEPA's environmental impact statement requirements. Environmental impact statements are most often challenged on the grounds that they do not sufficiently assess environmental impacts and their alternatives or have failed other procedural rules.

Problems for those involved with environmental litigation under NEPA include not only the financial resources required but also the highly contentious and divisive nature of court proceedings and decisions. NEPA lacked a provision for who would pay attorney fees; however, since the passage of the Equal Access to Justice Act in the early 1980s, NEPA plaintiffs or defendants can obtain payment of lawyers' fees by the loser if they win the case.

Several ingredients are common in every NEPA lawsuit: (1) a defendant, usually a federal agency proposing a major action or decision, (2) the environmental plaintiff(s) bringing suit against the agency, and (3) the actual NEPA provision that is under dispute. NEPA lawsuits may include on either or both sides: private parties; state or local agencies, or both; and municipal officials. In most cases, the latter would have a financial interest in the case and usually would back the federal agency's proposals. But that is not always the case. Over NEPA's thirty-year history, litigation has led to two main types of decisions: one interpreting NEPA policy mandates, the other establishing procedural requirements.

The founders envisioned Title I section 102 as a procedure that could enforce section 101's environmental values and goals in agency decision making. Section 102 was a vital part of NEPA's seamless web of intentions and the instruments designed to achieve those intentions. But however forthright section 101 sounds regarding NEPA's substantive goals, the compelling legal requirements of NEPA have been generally interpreted by the federal courts to be exclusively within the realm of section 102.[4] Unbeknownst to NEPA's founders during the legislative debates, section 102 would emerge as one of the most litigated measures in environmental law. A central legal and administrative question has been how Title I's goals ought to be included in the EIS and final decision. Was the new national policy to be a template against which agency policies could be compared?

Initially the founders' broad environmental goals appeared to be understood by the courts, as NEPA's long legal history was initiated. In 1971 the U.S. Court of Appeals for the District of Columbia ruled in *Calvert Cliffs' Coordinating Committee v. Atomic Energy Commission* that the environmental impact statement process must be implemented according to NEPA's principle statement of environmental policy.[5] In the *Calvert Cliffs* case, the normative proclamations of section 101 were given serious juridical weight.[6] This established a high threshold for federal agencies. A rigorously enforced NEPA is not without precedent in the federal courts. But beginning with the 1972 *Vermont Yankee v. NRDC*, the federal courts generally adopted Justice William Rehnquist's notion that NEPA is "essentially procedural." Now when the courts focus on procedural requirements, they do not decide whether the proposed federal action unduly harms the environment, unless it is related to the narrow legal issue at hand.

There are four important variables in every NEPA court case: (1) parties' standing in court, (2) reviewability, (3) standards for judicial review, and (4) judicial remedies. A plaintiff who wishes to bring suit against a governmental action must prove that (1) he or she has standing to sue and is the correct individual to bring suit, and (2) that the legal issues are suitable for the court to review. Reviewability concerns whether the issues raised by the plaintiff are appropriate for the particular court. How far and in what fashion the court is to review the cases is known as the standard of review. The options, or judicial remedies, available to courts, such as injunctions, are determined by the type of review a case receives.

Standing in Court

Legal standing is a broad threshold requirement that plaintiffs must satisfy in order to present their case in court. Standing in court is a twentieth-century judicial invention that helps the courts decide which cases to hear.

Those who do not have standing cannot litigate. The reader is referred elsewhere for a comprehensive history of the doctrine.[7] Here, we review the major cases that have framed the standing requirement.

Before plaintiffs can even seek to be recognized by a court as eligible to bring suit, they must exhaust all administrative remedies available to them. If plaintiffs do not participate in the public hearings and comment that are part of the EIS process, they may be disqualified from challenging an agency action or decision using NEPA. Nor is there provision for class-action suits. Furthermore, NEPA is structurally very different from most U.S. environmental laws in that it does not have a "citizens' suit" provision to allow citizens standing in court if they can show the agency neglected its legal obligation.

The standing doctrine stems from article 3 of the U.S. Constitution, which limits federal judicial power to considering "cases or controversies" coming from the Constitution, laws, and treaties of the United States as a whole. As Justice Brennan said in his dissent in *Allen v. Wright* (1984), "at a minimum, the standing requirement is not met unless the plaintiff has such a personal stake in the outcome of the controversy as to assure that concrete adverseness which sharpens the presentation of the issues upon which the court so largely depends."[8]

Significant legal debate exists over whether or not the "case and controversies" element of the U.S. Constitution actually restricts standing. The Supreme Court has insisted on three minimum aspects of article 3 standing requirements. First, the plaintiff must be able to demonstrate an "injury-in-fact."[9] Second, article 3 requires the injury to be traceable back to the contested action. Third, the plaintiff's injury must "likely be redressed by a favorable [court] decision."[10]

Besides the constitutional standing limitations, the Supreme Court has developed "prudential" requirements that further limit who is able to litigate cases before the Court.[11] There are three parts to these Court-imposed requirements. First, the plaintiff's claimed injury cannot be a general grievance that is "shared in substantially equal measure by all or a large class of citizens." Second, the plaintiff "must assert his own legal rights or interests, and cannot rest his claim to relief on the legal rights or interests of third parties."[12] Third, the plaintiff's argument must lie within the "zone of interests" to be protected by the relevant statute or constitutional provision.[13]

These prudential standing requirements are less relevant when Congress inserts a "citizens' suit" provision into its legislation that expressly authorizes standing.[14] The citizen suit provision grants legal standing for any injured party, subject to article 3 limitations, to bring a case under the statute in any relevant dispute. NEPA does not contain a citizen suit provision to enforce the act; therefore, plaintiffs must prove they have standing under the general standing requirements of the Administrative Procedures Act or other federal bases for standing, such as the Federal Declaratory Judgment. The APA dictates under section 10(a) that a person "adversely affected or aggrieved by agency action within the meaning of a relevant statute is entitled to judicial review thereof."[15] This two-part right was asserted by the Supreme Court in *Association of Data Processing Servicing Organizations v. Camp* (1970).[16] The *Data Processing* test requires the plaintiff seeking judicial review of an agency action to demonstrate two things: an "injury in fact" (economic or noneconomic) and an interest "arguably within the zone of interests to be protected or regulated" by the statute that the agency allegedly violated. As in *Sierra Club v. Morton,* discussed below, a "mere 'interest in the problem'" is insufficient by itself to confer standing.[17] To better demonstrate how the standing provision actually operates vis-à-vis environmental law and NEPA, we analyze the following case law.

Sierra Club v. Morton (1972)

This case was the first major environmental dispute in which the Supreme Court had occasion to consider legal standing. In this case, the Sierra Club environmental group sought a Court injunction in order to stop a Forest Service plan allowing Walt Disney Enterprises to build a $35-million resort in Mineral King Valley, in California's Sierra Nevada Mountains. In this case the Sierra Club, referring to the road that was to be built through Sequoia National Park, argued that the development would "destroy or otherwise adversely affect the scenery, natural and historic objects, and wildlife of the park and would impair the enjoyment of the park for future generations." The Court conceded that such damage could amount to "injury in fact" sufficient to find standing under section 10 of the Administrative Procedures Act and even noted that "aesthetic and environmental well-being, like economic well-being, is an important ingredient in the quality of life in our society, and the fact [that] the particular environmental interests are shared by the many rather than the few does not make them less deserving of legal protection through the judicial process." The Sierra Club did not claim it sustained an "injury in fact." Rather, the club based its lawsuit on the fact that it represented a broad public group seeking to enhance environmental quality.

The Court found that "injuring in fact" required more than an injury to some general societal interest and that there had to be a specific interest to the party seeking judicial review.[18] The Court, therefore, using the *Data Processing* test, concluded that the club did not establish an "injury-in-fact." The Court held that a long-standing interest in a problem was not enough to constitute an injury and thereby grant standing. Most important, however, the Court said the Sierra Club would have met the injury test if they had demonstrated that some of their members would be personally "injured" because they used the area for recreational purposes and would suffer an aesthetic injury of "spoiled" wilderness. In its pleading, the Sierra Club identified itself as doing business in San Francisco, California, since 1892 and documented a membership of approximately 78,000 nationally, of which approximately 27,000 members resided in the San Francisco Bay Area. The club also argued that for many years it exhibited a special interest in the conservation and sound management of national parks, game refuges, and forests in the United States and that one of the specific purposes of the club's initial creation had been to protect and conserve the Sierra Nevada Mountains. Nonetheless, the Supreme Court found that the failure to allege that any individual club members in any of their activities or pastimes would be negatively impacted meant that there was not an "injury in fact" as concerned the club, since any alleged injury would be to society at large—and such an injury cannot provide the basis for legal standing. Although this case may sound like a loss for the Sierra Club, it in fact was quite a victory for the environment. The Supreme Court basically said that while there was no standing in the Mineral King controversy for the Sierra Club, in the future all the club or similar organizations would have to do would be to allege that their members would be negatively affected by the activity in question. The subsequent effect of the Sierra Club ruling was to open the gates to a wide range of potential plaintiffs who could show that they would be personally injured in one way or another.

United States v. Students Challenging Regulatory Agency Procedure (SCRAP) (1973)

The Supreme Court applied its liberal *Sierra Club* standing doctrine in a subsequent case, known as *SCRAP I*.[19] This dispute involved a group of five law students who had organized themselves as an incorporated association in September, 1971, to "enhance the quality of the human environment for its members, and for all citizens," challenging the Interstate Commerce Commission's approval of an increase in railroad rates.[20] The plaintiffs claimed that the increased rates unfairly harmed opportunities to transport recycled materials and thus would encourage the use of raw materials, putting a further burden on nonrenewable resources. Increased rail rates would therefore reduce the recycling activities in their region, and litter would increase in the parks near the plaintiffs' homes and nationwide. Specifically, SCRAP argued that its members would suffer economic, aesthetic, or recreational harm as a direct result of negative environmental impacts caused by the new railroad rate structure. In addition, SCRAP argued that its members would have to pay more for finished products as a result of the new rate structure and that each of its members regularly used the forest, rivers, streams, and mountains around their legal residences in the Washington metropolitan area for camping, hiking, fishing, sightseeing, and other purposes. All these uses, SCRAP argued, would be adversely affected by the increased freight rates. In addition, SCRAP argued that the decrease in recycling that would result from the new freight rates would increase air pollution within the region and force SCRAP's members to pay increased taxes for the disposal of materials that would have to be recycled.

Despite this "attenuated line of causation," the Court reasoned that "to deny standing to persons who are in fact injured simply because many others are also injured, would mean that the most injurious and widespread Government actions could be questioned by nobody. We cannot accept that conclusion."[21] The Court held that injury is based on qualitative, not quantitative, factors. Consequently, the standing requirement was further liberalized for environmental plaintiffs.

Duke Power Co. v. Carolina Environmental Study Group, Inc. (1978)

Duke Power is another example of the Court's liberal interpretation of standing requirements. The plaintiffs in *Duke Power* (forty individuals who lived near the planned power plants, a labor organization, and the environmentalist Carolina Environmental Study Group) alleged that the Price-Anderson Act, which limits the liability of the nuclear industry for accident damages, encouraged the building of nuclear reactors. They claimed the statute was unconstitutional because if the plaintiffs ever incurred damages in excess of what was allowed by the statute, this would constitute an unlawful taking of property. Their contention was that because the Price-Anderson Act might very likely be found unconstitutional if invoked in the future, they were suffering environmental damage in the present. The plaintiffs also contended that construction of the nuclear plants would cause "injury in fact" due to the aesthetic and environmental consequences of the thermal pollution of two lakes in the vicinity of the proposed plants. The Court held that the "substantial likelihood" that the nuclear reactors near the plaintiffs' homes would not be built or operated in the absence of the Price-Anderson Act's liability limitations was a sufficient basis to establish an injury-in-fact and therefore the plaintiffs were granted standing.

Lujan v. National Wildlife Federation (1990)
In this case the National Wildlife Federation (NWF) challenged the Bureau of Land Management's (BLM) implementation of the Reagan administration's desire to open up parcels of federal land that were previously "withdrawn" from settlement, location, sale, or entry.[22] The plaintiffs attempted to comply with the previous standing requirements as set forth in *Sierra Club* and *SCRAP I* by showing that their members did in fact use this land and would be injured by the mining of the land.

However, in marked contrast to *Sierra Club* and *SCRAP I*, the Court ruled that the affidavits claiming members' land use were not sufficient because they did not contain "specific facts" showing use of precisely the land that would be affected by the BLM's reclassification.[23] Justice Antonin Scalia, writing the majority decision, held that the plaintiffs' use of land that was "in the vicinity" of the affected lands was not enough to grant standing.

A second component of Scalia's majority decision was that even if the affidavits were sufficient to grant standing, they would only be appropriate for the specific lands the members used. The Court reasoned that the NWF could not challenge the BLM's project as a whole but could use only piecemeal litigation.[24] The National Wildlife Federation had claimed that its members' "recreational use and aesthetic enjoyment" would be negatively impacted by the BLM's management practices. The court argued that there was no evidence that there were any specific use-of-enjoyment impacts and that a generalized injury could not be the grounds for standing unless it were connected to a particular activity on a particularly identified parcel. Consequently, the Court's ruling in *Lujan* severely restricted the standing requirements on plaintiffs seeking to challenge comprehensive abuses by federal agencies.

Lujan v. Defenders of Wildlife (1992)

In 1992, in *Lujan v. Defenders of Wildlife,* Justice Scalia wrote another opinion that had a significant impact on legal standing in environmental cases.[25] This is the leading operative legal standing case today. In *Lujan* environmental organizations sought standing to force the secretaries of Interior and Commerce to rescind regulations they had developed that removed the requirements of the Endangered Species Act from U.S. federal activities in foreign countries. Both secretaries initially developed a joint regulation extending Endangered Species Act section 7(a)(2) coverage to actions taken in foreign nations by the U.S. government. Subsequently a joint rule issued by the departments limited the section's geographic scope to the United States and the high seas.

Defenders of Wildlife and other environmentalist organizations sought to establish standing under several theories. But the court found that standing could only be established by showing that the environmentalist group members had suffered an injury-in-fact, that is, a concrete and particularized, actual or imminent invasion of a legally protected interest. Affidavits of members claiming they might or would visit the areas in question at some future time, and then be denied the opportunity to observe endangered animals, was not adequate to show an "imminent" injury.

It was held that the organizations could not validly assert standing based on (1) the organization members' affidavits, which did not support a finding of actual or imminent injury; (2) an "ecosystem nexus" theory, under which any person who uses any part of a contiguous ecosystem adversely affected by a funded activity would have standing to challenge that activity even if the activity was located a great distance away; (3) an "animal nexus" approach, whereby anyone who has an interest in studying or seeing endangered animals anywhere on the globe would have standing to challenge a federal decision that threatens such animals; (4) a "vocational nexus" approach, under which anyone with a professional interest in such animals would have standing to sue; or (5) the theory that the citizen-suit provision of the ESA (16 USCS 1540[g]) creates in all persons a procedural right to consultation under 7(a)(2), so that anyone can file suit in federal court to challenge the Secretary's failure to follow the assertedly correct consultative procedure, notwithstanding an inability to allege any discrete injury flowing from that failure.[26]

This decision meant that plaintiffs would no longer be able to show a generalized interest in a particular project but must show an actual injury in fact. Environmental groups would need to show that their members suffered specific injuries because of government action. In this particular case the environmentalist groups had not shown that one or more of their members would be directly affected by the agency action in question.

In addition, although governmental entities entitled to comment on EISs have standing to challenge another agency's noncompliance with NEPA, an agency without direct responsibility for promoting environmental programs does not have standing. Using NEPA and a handful of other laws and administrative rules, other entities granted standing to sue include a regional planning board when a federal agency action conflicts with local zoning laws, a state suing based on its *parens patriae* powers, and a corporation, a broadcasting company, and unions, depending on injury, degree of impact, and level of participation in the federal project.[27]

Friends of the Earth v. Laidlaw (2000)
In this case, environmentalists actually won a legal-standing case before a conservative Supreme Court. The case concerned a citizens' suit brought against a company that was allowed to be in violation of its Clean Water Act permit. The company later came into compliance, and the Fourth Circuit held that mooted the suit. The Supreme Court ruled, however, that there is a distinction between the issue of whether the plaintiff had standing and whether the case later became moot. So long as the defendant was in violation at the time the suit was brought, and so long as that violation injured the plaintiff, there is standing; the standing is not defeated by the defendant's later compliance. Nor does the defendant's later com-

pliance make the suit moot; the plaintiff is still entitled to seek civil penalties for the violations that were occurring as of and after the time the suit was brought.

Reviewability

Associated with NEPA's EIS procedural requirement is the act's own language stipulating that agencies must comply with the EIS process "to the fullest extent possible." This requirement has been one of the strongest legal tools for environmentalists to use when seeking to force compliance with NEPA. Yet despite its successes, this approach only focuses on the procedural aspects of an agency's decision and not on the actual outcome or policy derived from the procedures.

According to the 1983 Supreme Court, NEPA's "action-forcing" provision, the EIS requirement, has two major purposes. First, it "places upon an agency the obligation to consider every significant aspect of the environmental impact of a proposed project." Second, the EIS requirement "ensures that the agency will inform the public that it has indeed considered environmental concerns in its decision-making process."[28]

An EIS is necessary when "major Federal actions significantly affecting the quality of the human environment" are proposed.[29] The primary question the courts have struggled with is the nebulous "significant environmental impact" test. Determining which actions significantly affect the environment has been a constant problem for judicial review of NEPA. Early court decisions interpreted this language quite broadly. Some examples are judicial findings referring to situations where a project "may cause a significant degradation," "could have a significant effect," "arguably will have an adverse effect," or has a "potentially significant adverse effect."[30] Since the EIS came into existence, the threshold requirements for agency discretion in refusing to prepare an impact statement have been narrowed by the courts. There are four important considerations in the test for the necessity of an EIS: the action must be "major," "federal," and "significantly" affect the "human environment."[31]

NEPA case law is inconsistent on Congress' intent in including the word "major" within the statute. Its definition hinges on its association with the other words in the sentence, namely, "significantly affecting the human environment." The courts that read the two phrases independently of each other give to each its full review.[32] These courts base their determination of "major" on the amount of money and time involved with the action, as well as on the action's effect on the environment. But most courts interpret "major" directly in conjunction with "significantly."[33] The reasoning is that if a decision has a significant effect on the environment, the action is henceforth deemed major.[34]

Thus a 1974 Eighth Circuit of Appeals Court decision, *Minnesota Public Interest Research Group (MPIRG) v. Butz,* held that "major" is not an independent condition to be satisfied; instead it reinforces the meaning of "significantly affecting the human environment."[35] The *MPIRG* court rejected the Forest Service's argument that "major" was an exclusive requirement. Wisely, the court did not want to create a category of minor actions having a significant impact but requiring no impact statement. Instead, the court concluded that it would be contrary to NEPA's purpose to "separate the consideration of the magnitude of federal action from its impact on the environment."[36] The term "major" has been subsequently defined as any substantial commitment of environmental, monetary, or other resources.

An action is considered to be "federal" whenever a federal agency has some sort of control over the proposed project. The federal government can become involved through funding, contracting, licensing, or direct participation. Thus projects can be federal even though a private company may be the main actor. The same is true for a state or local government that is proposing a project to be funded by the federal government. In most cases this relationship is fairly clear and there is little dispute over this in the courts. An ongoing question, however, concerns NEPA's application in foreign lands.

The final threshold requirement, "significantly affecting the human environment," is one of NEPA's most contested clauses. This requirement includes two parts that need clarifying. First, what is a "significant" environmental impact? Second, what constitutes the "human environment"? NEPA's language clearly mandates that federal agencies recognize effects on more than the purely "natural environment." For example, in section 101, NEPA states that the nation must assure all Americans "safe, healthful, productive, and esthetically and culturally pleasing surroundings." Further, NEPA asserts the importance of preserving "important historic, cultural, and natural aspects of our national heritage."

The leading NEPA case defining "significant" is the 1972 *Hanly* decision in the Second Circuit Court of Appeals. In the first case, *Hanly v. Kleindeinst,* the court offered a two-part test that attempted to clarify the standards defining "significant."[37] First, the proposed action must be analyzed with respect to "the extent to which the action will cause adverse environmental effects in excess of those created by existing uses in the area." Second, "significant impact" is a function of "the absolute quantitative effects of the action itself, including the cumulative harm that results from its contribution to existing adverse conditions or uses in the area."[38] In a second *Hanly* case the court helped shape the definition of "human environment." *Hanly v. Mitchell* (1972) involved the construction of a jail in Manhattan. The plaintiffs argued that a new jail would not only increase air pollution but also adversely affect the aesthetics and safety of the local area. Using NEPA as a legal yardstick, the court held that building a jail would significantly affect the psychological and social well-being of the human environment and thus warranted an environmental impact statement.

In *Metropolitan Edison Co. v. People against Nuclear Energy* the Supreme Court clarified how psychological effects are complementary and not exclusive in terms of "significantly affecting the human environment."[39] A lower court held that the psychological stress of resuming operation of the Three Mile Island nuclear power plant would have a significant effect on the health of neighboring citizens and therefore an EIS was required. The Supreme Court affirmed this holding but held that the psychological effects must also be related to a significant change in the natural environment and can only qualify as part of the human environment if they are reasonably caused by a physical change.

Standards of Judicial Review: Dismantling Legislative Intent

Satisfying the standing and reviewability requirements is only the first step in NEPA litigation. Courts decide how to review based on the types of issues in the case. These disputes may be over questions of law, alleged facts, or procedural actions. The current judicial approach is typically deferential to narrower criteria in reviewing cases for all three circumstances. Thus once NEPA plaintiffs establish standing to sue, they have then to persuade courts to intervene with respect to the substance of the agency's contested action and not merely affirm agency decisions. Because NEPA does not contain a specific provision for judicial review of its procedural mandate, the EIS, much less for its substantive goals, federal courts routinely focus on the EIS under the Administrative Procedure Act's "arbitrary and capricious" standard as utilized by the court in the *Overton Park* case. But *Citizens to Preserve Overton Park v. Volpe* (1971), an early Supreme Court decision on NEPA, did create a broad precedent for reviewability in environmental cases, particularly in the application of NEPA.

In *Overton Park* the Supreme Court found that every federal agency is subject to judicial review except when there is explicit legislative language that prohibits review or where "agency action is committed to agency discretion by law."[40] Furthermore, unlike some environmental laws, NEPA does not contain a statute of limitations. The Supreme Court ruling in *Citizens to Preserve Overton Park v. Volpe* declared that, under the Administrative Procedures Act, courts must utilize a "hard-look" approach in evaluating defendant's actions and compliance with the NEPA process.[41]

The judicial review standard in APA section 706(2)(A) requires that the federal agency's final decision not be "arbitrary, capricious, an abuse of discretion, or otherwise not in accordance with law." The Court stated that the agency's "consideration of the relevant factors" and its "inquiry into the facts [are] to be searching and careful." Simply basing a decision on short-term economic criteria is not adequate. For example, if the Forest Service approved a new mine but did not adequately consider how allowing increased mining would affect the natural ecosystem, its decision in favor of mining would likely be considered "arbitrary and capricious" by the courts because the agency had not provided adequate information about wider adverse environmental effects and how to remedy them. Furthermore, agencies cannot claim ecological ignorance as an excuse for a decision that may have negative environmental effects. According to NEPA's section 102(2)(G), all federal agencies must "initiate and utilize ecological information in the planning and development of resource orientated projects." The judicial policy of reviewing agency decisions based on the factual merits is also known as the "substantial evidence" test, often characterized as the "hard look" approach.[42] Upholding Section 101's substantive call for the federal government to "use all practical means" to achieve environmental quality, some lower courts argue that "judicial action might be required if there was a significant potential for subversion of the substantive policies in NEPA." For example, in *Sierra Club v. Froehlke* (S.D. Texas 1973), the court required the Army Corps of Engineers to utilize a mitigation plan to maximize environmental values.[43]

However, *Overton* established the relatively weak "arbitrary and capricious" test for determining whether an agency acted properly with respect to the factual issues in a decision. If the agency's actions are accused of being capricious or arbitrary they are ultimately subject to judicial review. The difficulty, however, is the fact that this "test" is subject to diverse subjective interpretations by all involved. The Supreme Court concluded in *Overton* that "the ultimate standard of review is a narrow one [and] the court is not empowered to substitute its judgment for that of the agency."[44] Unfortunately, these mixed messages by the Supreme Court have not been clarified in later Court decisions. Generally, the issue of whether courts can review a federal agency's decisions has been treated in the affirmative. Whether the courts have the power to reverse agency decisions based on the merits of the case is another question. Indeed, while at times this test resembles a very intense review of an agency decision, the courts usually yield to agency expertise if the decision involves highly technical aspects deemed beyond the capacity of judicial review. Court interpretations of NEPA and the CEQ guidelines have left considerable room for agencies in implementing the substantive environmental values and national policy statements in NEPA's Title I.

Determining NEPA's substantive and procedural requirements was the critical question in *Calvert Cliffs' Coordinating Committee v. United States Atomic Energy Commission*, another early leading decision interpreting NEPA. In dicta presented in the first part of *Calvert Cliffs'*, Judge Skelly Wright of the District of Columbia Circuit Court of Appeals noted, "These cases are only the beginning of what promises to become a flood of new litigation—litigation seeking judicial assistance in protecting our national environment. Several recently enacted statutes attest to the commitment of the government to control, at long last, the destructive engine of material 'progress.'"[45]

The Atomic Energy Commission had developed rules implementing NEPA over a three-month period. The commission's regulations would have required that each applicant for an initial construction permit submit to the commission an "environmental report" presenting the applicant's assessment of the environmental impact of the planned facility and discussing any alternatives that might alter the impact. When construction was completed the applicant was required to submit another environmental report noting any changes that had taken place, including additional impacts, since filing the original report. These reports, although they were to "accompany" any formal review of an applicant's permit, were not to be brought into or considered in any hearing on the permit. The Atomic Energy Commission argued that they had prepared an adequate EIS document and any subsequent decision was at their discretion and should not be subject to judicial review.

The D.C. Circuit Court of Appeals disagreed, ruling that the EIS is more than a procedural requirement and could be reviewed on the basis of its quality and substance. The court found "the policies embodied in NEPA to be a good deal clearer and more demanding than does the commission." *Calvert Cliffs'* set the procedural bar for NEPA compliance, which remains to this day, and opened the doors for NEPA plaintiffs by stating that the Atomic Energy Commission's procedural interpretations of NEPA had "made a mockery of the Act." The court ruled that the statute's language did not allow for much agency flexibility, especially with regard to NEPA's "action-forcing mechanism," the EIS process. The court noted that NEPA did not provide "an escape hatch for foot-dragging agencies," nor were its "procedural requirements somehow 'discretionary.' Congress did not intend the act to be a paper tiger. Indeed, the requirement for environmental consideration to 'the fullest extent possible' sets a high standard for agencies, a standard which must be rigorously enforced by the reviewing courts." In this groundbreaking case, Judge Wright offered his unequivocal condemnation of agency noncompliance and asserted the power of the court to review administrative affairs under NEPA. Judge Wright declared that "the reviewing courts probably cannot reverse a substantive decision on its merits, under [NEPA's] Section 101, unless it can be shown that the actual balance of costs and benefits that was struck was arbitrary or clearly gave insufficient weight to environmental values. But if the decision was reached procedurally without individual consideration and balancing of environmental factors, conducted fully and in good faith, it is the responsibility of the courts to reverse."[46] The judicial precedent created here protects the integrity of NEPA's goals and procedures through nonmerit or procedural pleas.

In *Calvert Cliffs'* Judge Wright found that the AEC did not comply with NEPA to the "fullest extent possible" and therefore the court had the duty to enforce not just the procedural actions NEPA prescribes but also its intentions and values.[47] Expanding upon the law's "fullest extent possible" clause, the court noted that federal agencies are required to uphold the substantive goals of NEPA's section 101, using "all practical means." The court held that judicial review was constitutional if an agency violated NEPA's impact statement procedures and, by default, NEPA's substantive goals.

Even though the review was centered mostly on procedural violations, Judge Wright's decision is still one of the most inclusive, holistic court readings of NEPA. The *Calvert Cliffs'* decision was one of the early NEPA cases that enforced and reinforced the act's substantive measures through its procedural requirements. In many ways, it was a wake-up call to federal agencies that were not routinely implementing NEPA. Other courts followed the *Calvert Cliffs'* decision to reverse agency proposals and projects if they were not adequately researched and negotiated. In fact, Supreme Court Justice Thurgood Marshall, partly concurring and partly dissenting, in *Kleppe v. Sierra Club* (1975), maintained that the lower courts were the "source of NEPA's success" because they rigorously enforced the act.[48] The Supreme Court has subsequently reversed such lower court decisions. In contrast to the court's activist orientations regarding civil and property rights cases, the posture of the federal courts is generally recessive on the policies set forth in NEPA (with a few exceptions, notably the *Calvert Cliffs'* case). One explanation may be the specific rights and protections given to people (civil and property ownership) in the Constitution. To this extent, some have called for an amendment to the Constitution granting the right to a clean and healthy environment to every citizen of America. Subsequent Supreme Court decisions, beginning with *Vermont Yankee Nuclear Power Co. v. Natural Resources Defense Council* and *Stryker's Bay Neighborhood Council v. Karlen,* have not followed the *Calvert Cliffs'* finding that all of NEPA counted as judicially enforceable legislation.

In *Kleppe,* the Supreme Court quoted itself in holding that a court cannot "interject itself within the area of discretion of the executive as to the choice of the action to be taken." The Court went on to note, "Neither the statute nor its legislative history contemplates that a Court should substitute its judgment for that of the agency as to environmental consequences of its actions." This has led to a consistent pitfall for NEPA in the Supreme

Court: the Court's unwillingness to challenge the actual decisions made within other branches of government. If the minimal EIS procedures are met, the *Kleppe* Court concluded, "the only role for a court is to insure that the agency has considered the environmental consequences."[49] Thus the Court appears to be rubber-stamping agency "considerations" of NEPA's intent, values, and purpose even though environmental concerns may be marginalized in the agency's final decision.

Likewise, in *Vermont Yankee Nuclear Power Corp. v. Natural Resources Defense Council, Inc.* (1978), one of the first opinions curtailing NEPA, the Supreme Court held that the agency itself was in the best situation to decide its procedures.[50] The Court conceded that nuclear energy production poses severe potential health hazards and consequently potential adverse environmental effects that should be avoided. However, the Court argued, "Absent constitutional constraints or extremely compelling circumstances," administrative agencies should be given a free hand to develop their own rules of procedure and to implement those rules in ways that they see fit.[51] Consequently, the AEC and the Vermont Yankee Nuclear Power Corporation were allowed to ignore energy conservation and energy efficiency as an alternative to building a nuclear power plant. The Court held that the AEC had met the procedural requirements set forth in the Administrative Procedure Act and in NEPA, and could move forward with its permit to Vermont Yankee Nuclear Power Corporation to construct nuclear power plants. Justice Rehnquist articulated the Court's decision and his crabbed view of NEPA:

> NEPA does set forth significant substantive goals for the Nation, but its mandate to the agencies is essentially procedural. It is to ensure a fully informed and well-considered decision, not necessarily a decision the judges of the Court of Appeals or of this Court would have reached had they been members of the decision-making unit of the agency. Administrative decisions should be set aside in this context, as in every other, only for substantial procedural or substantive reasons as mandated by statute, not simply because the court is unhappy with the result reached.[52]

The Court specifically noted that the subsequent outcome of any correct procedural agency action would be enough, in the absence of some other flaw in the proceedings, to satisfy the agency's obligations under the Administrative Procedures Act and NEPA. The Court noted: "Thus, the adequacy of the record in this type of proceeding is not correlated directly to the type of procedural devices employed. . . . In sum, this . . . unwarranted judicial examination of procedural shortcomings of a rule-making proceeding can do nothing but seriously interfere with the process prescribed by Congress."[53]

The Supreme Court in *Vermont Yankee* did argue that the Atomic Energy Commission must "undertake its own preliminary investigation of the proffered alternative sufficient to reach a rational judgment whether it is worthy of detailed consideration in the EIS. Moreover, the commission must explain the basis for each conclusion that further consideration of a suggested alternative is unwarranted." But the Supreme Court went on to note that while the rationale for judicial intervention "is not entirely unappealing as an abstract proposition, as applied to this case we think it basically misconceives not only the scope of the agency's statutory responsibility, but also the nature of the administrative process, the thrust of the agency's decision, and the type of issues the interveners were trying to raise."[54]

In *Stryker's Bay Neighborhood Council, Inc. v. Karlen* the Supreme Court effectively killed any possibility of judicial enforcement of NEPA's substantive goals. In this case, the U.S. Department of Housing and Urban Development (HUD) proposed a site for low-income housing in New York City. Despite the objections of environmentalists, the Supreme Court ruled that HUD had met the procedural aspects of NEPA and had therefore complied with the entire statute. Reaffirming the *Vermont Yankee* decision, the Court stated:

> *Vermont Yankee* cuts sharply against the Court of Appeals conclusion [in *Stryker's Bay*] that an agency, in selecting a course of action, must elevate environmental concerns over other appropriate considerations. On the contrary, once an agency has made a decision subject to NEPA's procedural requirements, the only role for a court is to insure that the agency has considered the environmental consequences; it cannot interject itself within the area of discretion of the executive as to the choice of the action to be taken.[55]

In *Robertson v. Methow Valley Citizens Council* and *Marsh v. Oregon Natural Resources Council*, the Supreme Court continued to maintain that only

NEPA's procedural requirements are judicially enforceable.[56] In other words, NEPA's substantive requirements have meant virtually nothing to the more recent Supreme Court.

The lower courts had been less hesitant to overturn federal agency decisions, unlike the Supreme Court's 12-0 record against full NEPA enforcement. But Richard Goldsmith and William Banks have observed that as a consequence of the *Stryker's Bay* (1980) Supreme Court finding that NEPA's EIS requirement is essentially procedural, the lower courts "are enforcing NEPA with diminished rigor.... Under the influence of *Stryker's Bay*, some of the lower courts now seem to be reviewing agency action under NEPA far less closely than they review other types of agency action. This extreme deference to the federal bureaucracy invites the mockery of NEPA."[57] Judicial review continues to enforce only NEPA process and procedural questions. Agencies now have a clear idea how the courts will enforce NEPA and, not surprisingly, many agencies have tailored their decision making to meet only NEPA procedural steps.

Determining the Scope of the EIS

One problematic trademark of NEPA is its inconsistent level of judicially mandated administrative application and full compliance. David B. Firestone and Frank C. Reed documented five Supreme Court cases that required an EIS and five other Court cases in which an EIS was not required.[58] These excellent examples show the often nebulous criteria for the Court's deciding whether an EIS is required and reflect some of the disparities in EIS enforcement by the federal courts.

Examples of projects for which the federal courts have required an EIS include:

1. U.S. Department of Transportation regulations to increase accessibility of the handicapped to mass transportation[59]

2. U.S. Department of Housing and Urban Development loan of $3.5 million to construct a high-rise apartment building in an area in Portland, Oregon, containing no other high-rise buildings[60]

3. Army Corps of Engineers' designation of a new waste-dumping site in the waters of western Long Island Sound[61]

4. Trapping of red fox by the U.S. Fish and Wildlife Service in an effort to protect two endangered species of birds[62]

5. Participation of the United States in Mexican herbicide spraying of marijuana and poppy plants[63]

Examples of projects for which no EIS was required include:

1. U.S. Secretary of Transportation approving the crossing of an interstate highway by a huge strip-mining shovel[64]

2. HUD-insured loan of $3.7 million to construct a 272-unit apartment complex on fifteen acres in Houston, Texas[65]

3. Federal funding of a landfill containment project that was the result of a court order to remedy problems with the landfill[66]

4. U.S. Fish and Wildlife Service decision to enforce federal antibaiting requirements governing the taking of migratory waterfowl[67]

5. Aerial surveillance of federal lands for detection of marijuana growing[68]

Clearly, enforcement of NEPA's EIS requirements is subject to varying legal interpretations and decisions. The courts' discretionary interpretations of NEPA, specifically the EIS requirement, have disappointed some who feel that the courts should order federal agencies to uphold the more comprehensive substantive provisions of NEPA's declared purpose and goals. Determining what the EIS is going to discuss and when this must occur effectively determines the substance of alternatives and impacts to be considered.

Content of the EIS

The extent of the number, type, and scope of alternatives has been a major issue in NEPA litigation. The CEQ requirements assert that "the EIS must state how the alternatives in it and decisions based on it will or will not achieve the requirements of Title I of NEPA; the range of alternatives discussed in environmental impact statements shall encompass those to be considered by the ultimate agency decision maker."[69] The courts, as other than experts in administrative particulars and technical details, have been reluctant to rule on the adequacy of EIS preparation. Settling on a midrange level of judicial review, many courts now use the "reasonableness" standard for determining the adequacy of alternatives discussed. If the agency proves it has undertaken a "good faith" effort to identify all the alternatives, the courts have tended to defer to the agencies.

In the leading "reasonableness" case, *NRDC v. Morton* (1972), another of Judge Skelly Wright's decisions, the appeals court held that the Department of Interior did not address all the relevant alternatives to offshore drilling, particularly the option of eliminating oil import quotas, and therefore it was in violation of NEPA's requirements. The Department of Interior contended that this option was beyond the department's jurisdiction because it did not have the power to implement this alternative. The court disagreed, and without commenting on what the department's final choice should be, the court held that the Department of Interior had not followed the proper EIS procedures for the alternatives to be discussed.

In *Vermont Yankee Nuclear Power Corp. v. NRDC* (1978) and more recently in *Robertson v. Methow Valley Citizens Council* (1989), the Supreme Court used the "reasonableness" standard to deny the environmental plaintiffs' claim that the respective agencies did not properly address all the alternatives and their consequences.[70] In *Vermont Yankee* the Court held that the Atomic Energy Commission adequately discussed "energy conservation" for building more nuclear power plants, even though this was a minuscule part of their EIS. The *Robertson* decision, written by Chief Justice Rehnquist, rejected the CEQ's worst-case scenario requirement for discussing the consequences of the alternatives to the 100 percent elimination of a mule deer herd. A bigger blow to NEPA and congressional intent was the Court's *Robertson* holding that even if the Forest Service had considered such alternatives, they still could issue a permit for a ski resort and be within NEPA's mandate. In the majority opinion, Chief Justice Rehnquist maintained that "the agency is not constrained by NEPA from deciding that other values outweigh the environmental costs. . . . Other statutes may impose substantive environmental obligations on federal agencies, but NEPA merely prohibits uninformed—rather than unwise—agency action."[71]

The Rehnquist interpretation of NEPA in *Robertson* as requiring also only a minimal level of public participation is fundamentally contradictory to the act's legislative content and the CEQ literature. Rehnquist is correct in saying NEPA prohibits uninformed agency decision making, but this is not "merely" what the three-page act and subsequent CEQ regulations and instructions require the federal government to do. In section 1500.1(c) of the 1978 CEQ Regulations, it reads, "Ultimately, of course, it is not better documents but better decisions that count. NEPA's purpose is not to generate paperwork—even excellent paperwork—but to foster excellent action. The NEPA process is intended to help public officials make decisions that are based on understanding of environmental consequences, and take actions that protect, restore, and enhance the environment. These regulations provide the direction to achieve this purpose." Further, a part of the next section clearly offers CEQ's view of what agency decisions ought to be about: "Use all practicable means, consistent with the requirements of the Act and other essential considerations of national policy, to restore and enhance the quality of the human environment and avoid or minimize any possible adverse effects of their actions upon the quality of the human environment."[72] Moreover, to understand the mandate of NEPA the CEQ states that "the provisions of the Act and of these regulations must be read together as a whole in order to comply with the spirit and letter of the law." Finally, in section 1502.2(d) of the CEQ regulations: "Environmental impact statements shall state how alternatives considered in it and decisions based on it will or will not achieve the requirements of Sections 101 and 102(1) of the Act and other environmental laws and policies."[73]

Conclusion

The Supreme Court has consistently weakened the comprehensive environmental mandate in NEPA. The authors of NEPA did not write the law simply to change agency procedures for the sake of changing them. The EIS was intended to be a tool to enforce larger NEPA policy goals, most important the paragraph in section 101 that states NEPA's fundamental purpose, "to promote efforts which will prevent or eliminate damage to the environment." The goal was to move the administrative process toward a decision-making framework that would be able to account for environmental issues previously unconsidered by federal decision makers. However, NEPA's substantive mandates have been undermined by the Supreme Court in its consistent view that only section 102 is enforceable.

In its thirty years of existence, NEPA has barely scratched the surface of our nation's and globe's most pressing environmental questions, such as population growth and resource depletion. Yet as Andrews noted in 1976, NEPA "may well have been the best instrument that its sponsors in the Congress could have created at the time. NEPA's purposes could not have been enacted by frontal challenge to the missions of existing agencies—those missions were and are supported by powerful constituencies not only in the agencies but [also] in lobbies of beneficiaries and in the congressional committee structure."[74] Although NEPA's EIS provision is an especially adequate tool to implement the act, the Supreme Court has failed to see the intersection between the action required and the values and visions that were to inform the action-forcing procedure. Because the federal courts treated NEPA law and executive implementation through a doctrine of agency discretion, and treated the EIS as an exercise in document production only, "the number of NEPA cases declined dramatically" in the 1980s "as environmental groups turned their resources to pollution control issues."[75]

CHAPTER 7

NEPA's Legacy, NEPA's Future

This book has worked to demonstrate that the practice of implementing NEPA often neglects the law's comprehensive national values and applications. The authors of NEPA clearly intended the act to be something more than a procedural paper chase or, as Judge Skelly Wright put it, a paper tiger. Mark Sagoff contended that NEPA's architects created the law to ensure "policy goals [that] are explicitly ethical."[1] Robert Bartlett argued that NEPA instituted a new ecological rationality that represented "a way of thinking about actions, about organizations, and about ultimate ends or values."[2] NEPA's legislative history makes evident Congress's anticipation that NEPA's policy goals and the CEQ would play a more prominent role than they have in the act's implementation. This final chapter reviews NEPA's status in environmental law today and assesses several suggestions for improving the process and enforcement of the act.

Evaluating NEPA

Riding the crest of the late 1960s, NEPA called for a unique paradigm shift in policy making. "No previous statute had dealt in such sweeping terms with relationships between American society and its environment; no other statute had cut across departmental lines to modify or redirect so fundamentally the priorities and criteria of agency decision making."[3] NEPA's declarations of environmental policy integrated into the political landscape interagency environmental planning, ecosystem awareness, future generational rights, recycling, renewable resources, and the valuing of nonquantifiable ecological values. While statutes are rarely fully effective, NEPA certainly shook the federal government's decision-making foundation.[4]

Changing the structure, policy, or process of the federal government is a monumental task—one usually occurring in fits and starts over time. As Lynton Caldwell succinctly laments:

> NEPA activates value conflicts formerly repressed or latent in American society. But the disturbing potential of the Act is greater than its practical effect thus far because its possibilities have not been fully utilized. Presidents, with the exception of actions by Richard Nixon during the first months following enactment, have failed to give it vigorous support. The courts, moreover, have been ambivalent with respect to the practical significance of its substantive provisions (Section 101). The Congress has underfunded the Council for Environmental Quality (in deference to presidential priorities) and no president, to date, has chosen to use the CEQ as an instrument of policy, or permitted it to use fully its statutory powers.[5]

It also appears that Congress did not foresee the extensive role the federal courts would play in interpreting and enforcing NEPA. Interestingly, it is the courts, not the environmental or scientific community, that have elevated the EIS requirement to its predominant status in environmental planning. However, the courts concomitantly have lessened the impact of the fundamental and substantive provisions of the law (and thus also of the EIS). This paradoxical effect of the courts' response to NEPA, especially that of the Supreme Court, is rooted in the courts' historical unwillingness to challenge the discretionary judgment of federal agencies on environmental matters.

The procedural reforms mandated by NEPA have no doubt improved the quality and quantity of environmental planning throughout the federal agencies. Instituting a mechanism for more rational planning regarding the environment is the chief function and benefit of NEPA and of the EIS process in particular. The EIS forces agencies to disclose their plans and proposals and to allow the public an opportunity to comment on the agencies' plans. The EIS process is also a catalyst for interagency coordination and cooperation. NEPA forces agencies to investigate all the consequences of their actions and justify their actions with respect to the costs and benefits of those actions. As NEPA architect Lynton Caldwell stated, "Rationality in the sense of informed logical thought cannot guarantee the attainment of the desired outcome, but may increase its probability." But he continued, "That which appears at the moment to be rational for the individual [or agency] may not, in the long run, be rational for society."[6] In any case, meeting the procedural requirements of the EIS process does not by itself fulfill the goals and intentions of NEPA.

Compared to most resource- or issue-specific environmental regulations, NEPA's success is difficult to measure accurately. To accurately measure NEPA's effect, one would have to account for the hundreds, perhaps thousands of ecologically damaging projects that were never built. Yet attempts to evaluate NEPA's impact on both environmental politics and environmental law are numerous and varied. Many social scientists have documented ways NEPA has affected the bureaucracy.[7] The literature evaluating NEPA often falls within the boundaries of the different social science disciplines. For example, mainstream economists rarely find NEPA a constructive piece of legislation. Consider the comments from one leading economist: "The principle effect has been to slow passage of new legislation, the enactment of agency decisions, and the commencement of private-sector projects. . . . The . . . impact statements are so voluminous that no one considers or even reads them, much less attempts to modify decisions on the basis of their findings." Yet the claim that NEPA produces undesirable delays in agency decisions has simply not been supported by evidence. According to Serge Taylor's analysis of EIS-related litigation from 1970 to 1981, only 10 percent of all EISs ended in litigation.[8] Today this figure is even smaller. The exact extent to which NEPA has affected the federal government is debatable and difficult to measure.

While NEPA's history is settled, its future evolutionary course will be influenced by choices made today. To restore the quality of the law's implementation, a renaissance—a reincarnation of NEPA's values and visions—is needed for an ecologically sustainable twenty-first century. Following are suggestions that have been offered for improving the act's interpretation and implementation.

Proposals for Improving NEPA

The lack of complete integration of or support for environmental policy by federal agencies has been discussed by the CEQ, agencies, and scholars. Several administrative and academic studies of NEPA have been undertaken. Among them, Caldwell's investigatory study of ways to improve the scientific method and substance of the EIS found that a significant difficulty with implementing NEPA goals was not attributable to NEPA or the EIS itself but instead to lack of agency enthusiasm for NEPA objectives. Caldwell suggested that comprehensive NEPA implementation could be helped by a more vigorous CEQ and by louder NEPA enthusiasts sitting on congressional committees with jurisdiction over environmental issues and policies.[9] NEPA does not compel agencies to base their decisions on EIS findings, so any increase in agency response to substantive NEPA goals and intentions is often minimal.

Several ways of ensuring compliance with NEPA goals have been suggested. NEPA could use revitalization and sharper regulatory teeth to compel ecological justifications for agency action. Because environmental issues enjoy little constitutional, presidential, or agency support or leverage, Caldwell also suggested a constitutional amendment for the environment.[10] In a 1998 *Harvard Environmental Law Review* article, Caldwell argued that three reasons justify considering a constitutional amendment on the environment.

> *First,* an examination of the arguments for and against an amendment would open the way for a broad appraisal of the relative importance, effects, and limitations of environmental policy generally, and NEPA in particular. It would occasion a debate on the propriety of its inclusion in the Constitution, as compared with other amendments. *Second,* the debate over an environmental amendment could lead to examination of the role of law in relation to foreseeable environmental risks and their unwanted consequences with which society is presently unprepared to cope. *Third,* the issue raises the question of which policies are appropriate for a written constitution that is intended to declare the fundamental responsibilities and limitations of government. The low visibility of the environmental goals and principles declared

under Section 101(b) of NEPA, the narrow construction of NEPA by the Supreme Court, and the ambiguity of presidential attitudes toward NEPA and the CEQ have reinforced an effort—already underway before NEPA—to confer constitutional status to environmental protection equal to property rights and civil rights.[11]

Many other law review contributors have also presented suggestions for changing NEPA implementation and enforcement practices. For example, Philip Ferester studied state environmental impact laws—known as "little NEPAs" because they are modeled after NEPA—and suggested amending NEPA to create a more explicit link between its substantive policies and procedural mechanism than it presently has. He specifically suggested changing NEPA section 105, which currently reads: "The policies and goals set forth in this chapter are supplementary to those set forth in existing authorizations of Federal agencies." Based largely on the state of Washington's NEPA-like law, Ferester recommended changing section 105 to: "Any governmental action may be conditioned or denied pursuant to the policies and goals set forth in this chapter. Denials must be based upon clearly identified adverse environmental effects disclosed through an environmental impact statement prepared under section 102(2)(C)."[12]

According to the CEQ, among the most prominent recommendations for improving NEPA arising out of a 1997 NEPA effectiveness study, is the need for "adaptive environmental management." NEPA has succeeded in modifying proposals and mitigating adverse environmental effects before they occur. However, the functioning of ecosystems is in constant flux and therefore NEPA's reliance on ecological predictions needs to be augmented through continued monitoring to confirm that these impact predictions and their mitigation measures are correct, and to account for unintended consequences. As the CEQ report maintained, when the environment is not going to be permanently damaged, when a project may be modified once started, and when there are opportunities to improve past environmental damage, "an adaptive environmental management approach may be the best means of attaining both NEPA's goals and an agency's mission."[13]

The Council on Environmental Quality

The future role for the CEQ itself is uncertain. The president's top advisers on the environment, the economy, national security, and trade are all appropriately housed within the executive office of the president (EOP), but the CEQ is often the lonely voice for environmental quality. As Vig and Kraft maintain, "the CEQ is [a] spectacular example of institutional neglect or destruction."[14] One may hope that its role within the executive office will become better understood and supported.

Despite the fact that article 2, section 3 of the Constitution requires that the president "faithfully execute" the nation's laws, NEPA's administrative fate, in terms of presidential support, is quite negative. Although Congress clearly called for the creation of a three-person Council on Environmental Quality, no president since 1980 has treated the CEQ as a *council*, appointing only a chairman, and from 1993 to 1995 not even a chairman. Every administration since President Jimmy Carter's has discussed abolishing the CEQ.[15]

When presidents refuse to support the CEQ ideologically and financially, they set it up to fail. Reagan's administration seriously marginalized the CEQ. In fact, the CEQ's budget fell from $3.1 million in 1980 to $700,000 in 1985.[16] According to Dinah Bear, general council of the CEQ, "President Bush strengthened CEQ's resources a great deal and restored it to some degree to the policy role that was absent in the Reagan years."[17] President Bush appointed Michael Deland as CEQ chairman, whose goal was to "restore what he calls a 'moribund' agency." By most accounts he was successful. CEQ staff and resources were more than doubled in the Bush Administration. Deland worked in close proximity to the president and served as one of Bush's top advisors on environmental affairs.[18] President Clinton followed Bush's lead, by also appointing strong environmental advocates to the position of CEQ chair. From 1992 to 1997, Kathleen A. McGinty was the first female to chair the position. McGinty, like Deland, wasn't as visible as the EPA Commissioner, but she played a crucial role in environmental policy formation and enforcement in the Clinton-Gore Administration. George T. Frampton, appointed in 1997 to CEQ chair, is past president of the Wilderness Society, and served as senior environmental policy advisor to President Clinton and Vice President Gore.

In 1993 the Clinton administration announced its intention to abolish the CEQ and transfer NEPA oversight to the EPA.[19] Clinton was the second president to propose eliminating the CEQ. Although this proposal was tabled, it illuminated a number of interesting issues.

Perhaps one reason the CEQ has so often come under the budget-cutting knife is the lack of understanding and networking between mainstream environmental groups and the CEQ. For example, in April, 1993, when the Senate Committee on Environment and Public Works held a hearing on abolishing the Council on Environmental Quality, few environmental groups voiced opposition to this proposal.[20] Since the CEQ's elimination was tied to giving the EPA Commissioner a cabinet-level post, environmental groups apparently hoped that by granting the EPA full cabinet status, environmental protection would be enhanced. While their intentions of strengthening the environment's voice in the executive branch are benign, their understanding of NEPA and the purpose of the CEQ is primitive.

While the CEQ can be compared with the Council of Economic Advisors (CEA) in terms of organizational formats, no one, regardless of political orientation, can conceive of eliminating the CEA. The contrast between the CEA and CEQ is significant because, while their organizational model and statutory mandate are similar, the saliency of economic information and analysis, in the eyes of policy elites, is very high, especially compared to that for ecology. However, since NEPA's founders believed the economy is affected by our environment and vice versa, environmental quality was also given executive-office status.

Demonstrating a very narrow understanding of the world (and word), some continue to assert that the environment is a "special issue" and often a political windfall for an elite group of environmentalists who want clean rivers to go fly-fishing in, and who use the latest goods from places like L. L. Bean and Orvis. The corporate controlled mainstream media treat the environment as something separate from jobs, health, psyches, and national security. This view of ecology and the environment is common and pigeonholes the environment as just another ordinary political issue. The creators of NEPA understood environmental quality to be fundamental to human health and the health of the cosmos. CEQ is in the executive office so the council would not be forced to be judged by and compete with its peers as just another cabinet-level department. Instead, from within the EOP the CEQ was designed to monitor the whole administration with more objectivity and less institutional jealousy and to recommend policies within that context. Recommending that the environment be given a cabinet position may boast EPA's power, for instance, but it also is a reflection of the all-too-popular view that the environment represents a special clientele. In reality environmental issues are often a classic example of a general public good—one in which no one is excluded from the benefits and costs associated with environmental policy, especially if judged from a bio-regional or ecosystem perspective.

Of course, the president of the United States is faced with a multitude of demands, many inconsistent with one another, and must attempt to strike a balance among a cacophony of roles. For example, as the top elected official in his political party he is the de facto leader of his party. This role entails articulating goals for the party (and nation) and in essence making choices that benefit his political party. As a public official and the chief executive of the country, the president must attend to the duties of the presidency set forth in article 2 of the Constitution. Of utmost importance for this study is not just the president's "oath or affirmation: I do solemnly swear (or affirm) that I will faithfully execute the office of President," but that as such "he shall take care that the laws be faithfully executed." But beginning with President Nixon and continuing right through President Clinton's administration, NEPA's goals and declarations have received scant attention and support by the chief executive. Although Dan Dreyfus and Helen Ingram wrote in 1976 that the "impact of the Act was enhanced beyond initial expectations," it would appear that the president, as well as Congress, seek to reverse that.[21]

When the president chooses to ignore or sidestep NEPA, it is hardly surprising that federal agencies proceed to do the same. Having a president give NEPA the appropriate platform it deserves would surely aid in its being effectively approved. The Council on Environmental Policy continues to be underfunded and understaffed, and presidential support for the CEQ and the act also continues to be minimal. All this needs to change if NEPA is to be fully and effectively implemented, ensuring that a broad range of environmental considerations will be part of agency decision making.

The EIS

The disappointments and limitations of NEPA aside, there is little doubt that the EIS process has improved environmental decision making in significant ways.[22] NEPA forces policy makers to think clearly about their goals and to examine alternative means of achieving those goals. NEPA mandates public participation which democratizes administrative decision making to some extent. Because of NEPA, federal decisions are evaluated more carefully, with input from more ordinary but informed people, in a much more public manner than had previously been the case. As the Council on Environmental Quality reported in 1997, NEPA "has made agencies take a hard look at the potential environmental consequences of their actions, and . . . [has directed] federal agencies to open their doors, bring the public in, and offer genuine opportunities for participation and collaboration in decision making."[23] Though NEPA lacks forceful and enforceable substantive teeth, the open debate and evaluation under NEPA have prevented many questionable projects from proceeding.

The CEQ's *Effectiveness Study,* completed in 1997, identified five factors as important to NEPA's success: (1) early implementation of the planning process, (2) community outreach that facilitates open and effective dialogue with the public, (3) coordination between agencies that helps agencies share information, (4) cross-disciplinary analysis using various sources of site-based information, and (5) solid but flexible science management. These excellent suggestions, if thoroughly implemented, would go a long way toward creating the kind of NEPA implementation long overdue.

It is generally agreed that NEPA's greatest effect on the administrative state resides in its encouraging the internalizing of a mechanism for social and environmental change. The EIS process creates opportunities and incentives for individuals to "put their imprint on policy change by inventing and building coalitions, by making the case for change on the merits, and, as Lynton Caldwell first imagined they would, by developing and affirming in EIS their environmental values."[24] Successful environmental impact assessment mandates the consideration of values of a wide variety of parties previously not required in agency decision making. The act has opened up federal decision making to the public and, as such, has significantly changed the relationships among organizations—both public and private.

Many scholars have nevertheless asserted the need for more formal controls and a clearer legal mandate for EIS application. Reviewing environmental impact assessment in North America and western Europe, William V. Kennedy concluded that environmental impact assessment "works best when it is instituted in a formal-explicit way. That is to say, it works when there is a specific legal requirement for its application, where an environmental impact statement is prepared, and where authorities are accountable for taking its results into consideration in decision making." In their 1996 annual report, the CEQ reported that "over the years, some federal managers have learned to 'comply' with NEPA by preparing environmental impact statements that will pass muster with the courts."[25] When the courts only enforce the paperwork behind NEPA and neglect the principles of the law, there is often a strong judicial disincentive to integrate NEPA's core values into an agency's mission if they conflict.

In addition to the lack of substantive impact, scholars have identified other problems with the NEPA process as currently applied. For example, according to Ray Clark, former senior policy analyst with the CEQ, "Many environmental impact statements are too long, take too long to prepare, cost too much, and many times do too little to protect the environment. Some EISs are prepared to justify decisions already made, many agencies fail to monitor during and after the project, some agencies do not provide adequate public involvement, and few agencies assess the cumulative effects of an action."[26] When the CEQ limits on length are not adhered to, critics of the EIS process point out, excessive length leads to excessive costs and the production of documents that are too technical for the layperson to understand.[27] From a high in 1973 of around 2000 a year, the number of EISs filed per year has dropped to around 500 (beginning in mid 1980s). This is partly due to increased costs, page lengths, and time for preparation, as well as the federal courts' precedence of allowing agencies discretion within the EIS process. In addition, fewer EISs are filed today due to the increased use of "mitigated" Environmental Assessments and "mitigated" FONSIs (Finding of No Significant Impact, a ruling that eliminates the need for EIS preparation) and categorical exclusions.[28] When disputing parties compromise prior to EIS preparation, most litigation and other costs are significantly reduced. While this is sometimes very desirable, the avoidance of EIS preparation can result in impacts, particularly cumulative impacts, that are neglected. In addition, the study of other alternatives to the proposed project is also minimized, because while that is a fundamental part of an EIS, it is not in an EA. The tragic irony of the contemporary NEPA process is that an EIS of whatever length may be written that describes an activity with horrendous environmental consequences and includes the negative comments of hundreds of outraged citizens, while still satisfying the court-driven procedural process.

One valuable suggestion is to phase out, or at least curtail, the use of private EIS consultants who are in the business to do their client's bidding. As Ray Clark argued, "Too much reliance on outsiders to conduct scoping meetings and prepare NEPA analyses, without appropriate oversight from federal officials, can lead to a perfunctory paper-compliance approach to the process." The contracting of EIS duties to private firms invites serious conflict of interest questions. As former Department of Interior attorney and NEPA scholar Joseph Sax explained, "Don't expect hired experts to undermine their employers."[29] This rule, coupled with cozy and entrenched relationships between governmental agencies and their traditional friends, necessitates reforming how EISs are prepared.

So how might NEPA's implementation be amended to provide the teeth that would prevent decisions detrimental to the environment? Besides the recommendations previously articulated, two other modest possibilities have some promise. First, the integration of risk assessment in the NEPA process could be done in such a way as to foster substantive environmental decisions. Second, social, cultural, and economic impact analysis could be strengthened.

With regard to risk assessment, when a certain activity causes X risk of Y happening, then the activity would be limited or banned. We might, further, determine that carcinogenic risks of one in ten thousand exposures or less is against federal law. The EIS process could determine the level of exposure and the risk associated with that exposure. If the exposure is over the desired threshold, the activity would be more heavily regulated. Risk management seeks to limit exposure to toxic agents in such a way as to limit negative impacts.

The EPA has already developed guidelines for carcinogenic risk assessment designed to evaluate the nature and the magnitude of risks associated with exposure.[30] Using EPA guidelines, or others designed specifically for this purpose, risk assessment and management could be used in a way that would guide, limit, or prohibit an activity that had carcinogenic or other negative impacts. There are, however, a number of problems with this approach. First, of the more than sixty thousand chemicals in use, only about one thousand have been examined in enough detail to make any risk assessment to exposure acceptably accurate. The cost is staggering for testing the many thousands of chemicals currently in use for their human toxicity in a way that allows a reliable risk assessment. In addition, latency periods, the synergistic effects of chemicals within our bodies, and the unique risks of exposure for certain more vulnerable sectors of the population all make risk assessment very difficult. Finally, most projects subject to EIS requirements do not involve the release of anything into the atmosphere, water, soil, food, and so on, making risk assessment of limited value.

Social, cultural, and economic impacts have always been required in the EIS process, but they often are limited, downplayed, or ignored. One quantitative content analysis of EISs found that 86.5 percent had "no social research method or technique."[31] To the extent that the social sciences are used in the EIS process, they usually focus on specific economic and technical considerations, ignoring broader social impacts.[32] One possible change would be a strengthening of NEPA procedural requirements, including requiring a more detailed examination of social and intergenerational impacts.

Reforming the EIS process involves providing better social, cultural, and economic impact analysis. The statutory requirements for social impact analysis are quite clear. Section 101 of NEPA identifies among its purposes "to fulfill the social, economic, and other requirements" of U.S. citizens. Section 102(2)(A) requires "integrated use of the natural and social sciences in decisionmaking which may have an impact on [human] environment."[33] CEQ guidelines for implementing NEPA reinforce these requirements. Social impacts include "all social and cultural consequences to human populations of any public or private actions that alter the ways in which people live, work, play, relate to one another, organize to meet their needs, and generally cope as members of society." After the decision was made to build the Alaskan pipeline in 1973, an Inuit tribal chief was quoted as poignantly saying, "Now that we have dealt with the problem of the permafrost and the caribou and what to do with hot oil, what about changes in the customs and ways of my people?"[34]

The Council on Environmental Quality as well as various commentators have pressed for increased analysis of social and economic impacts.[35] Improved social, cultural, and economic impact analysis would certainly enhance the EIS process and would strengthen the link between the EIS and substantive NEPA goals. In those cases where social impacts have been ignored, the courts have merely, and expectedly, required that they be addressed (i.e., that the EIS procedure be followed). Furthermore, there are very few cases where it can be shown that the social impact analysis of an EIS has actually made a difference in the decision-making process.[36]

In 1994 President Clinton issued Executive Order 12898 "Federal Actions to Address Environmental Justice in Minority Populations and Low-Income Populations," which among other things, requires that federal agencies make it part of their mission to identify and address disproportionately high adverse negative environmental impacts on minority and low-income populations.[37] In the 1997 publication "Environmental Justice Guidance under the National Environmental Policy Act," the CEQ issued some very helpful suggestions for integrating President Clinton's Executive Order 12898. For example, agencies are encouraged to seek public participation through a variety of means beyond the traditional public hearing method to ensure participation from a wide cross-section of the public. In sum, the 1997 CEQ guidance recommends that agencies include environmental justice considerations throughout the EIS process and make it easier for impacted communities to participate (e.g. have bi-lingual documents and speakers).[38]

It is entirely possible that in the future we may look back on Executive Order 12898 and find that the EIS process responded by merely identifying negatively impacted populations, without in fact having actually reduced or much less avoided those negative impacts on the populations. In short, "environmental justice," like the other social requirements of section 102(2)(A), may be given short shrift in the EIS process. President Clinton's Executive Order 12898 needs further executive leadership. One primary debate will be how to measure "disproportionate impact to minorities and low-income populations." It remains to be seen how President George W. Bush will enforce environmental policies, but based on his campaign, he will most likely be very reticent about including NEPA and environmental justice on his policy agenda. So while these two reforms— improved risk and social impact assessment—would undoubtedly improve the EIS process, they would not provide the teeth that the authors of NEPA hoped the act would have, either because the new regulation cannot (in the case of risk assessment) or would not (in the case of social impact assessment) reduce negative effects of action affecting the environment.

Conclusion

As our country makes the transition into the twenty-first century, we need to reinvigorate environmental assessment practices and NEPA's value paradigm to better coordinate and harmonize human life with ecological processes. The architects of NEPA provided the federal government with the necessary tools for environmental planning. However, as one commentator suggested, "What was a major step forward in 1969 is woefully out of synch with the important and inescapable environmental needs this country must address in the twenty-first century." Christopher Wood, in a comparative study of the environmental impact assessment process (primarily in the United States, Europe, Canada, Australia, and New Zealand) concluded that the EIS process in the United States had several shortcomings, but the predominant one was a "lack of centrality to decision making . . . and to the mitigation and monitoring of impacts."[39]

Among the biggest problems with NEPA's effectiveness is not the language of the statute, but rather the lack of judicial and presidential enforcement of NEPA policy goals, and the lack of integrated and cumulative NEPA decision-making processes. The CEQ attempts to fulfill its mandate of assisting agencies and providing reports on environmental quality, but almost every sector of the federal government could improve its compliance with the letter and spirit of the law. However, without sufficient resources and presidential support, the CEQ and EPA can only do so much to support NEPA's implementation.

Despite all the problems associated with NEPA, it is clearly a powerful statute with a significant impact and a vast potential. Considering its real and potential effect on federal agencies and the fact that it serves as a catalyst for state laws and the laws of other countries that mirror NEPA, perhaps Senator Jackson was correct when he stated that NEPA "is the most important and far-reaching environmental and conservation measure ever enacted by the Congress."[40] As the CEQ puts it, "the challenge of harmonizing our economic, environmental, and social aspirations has put NEPA at the forefront of our nation's efforts to protect the environment."[41] This bold step forward was especially remarkable in a legislative body built upon incremental policy making usually heavily influenced by economic rather than ecological goals. Indeed, nonincremental policy options are available today that may provide long-term solutions to many environmental problems. Reinterpreting NEPA as a text that commands responsive and responsible federal planning and action will strengthen the quest for holistic, ecologically orientated decisions within the federal government.

But NEPA is not a panacea for administrative efficiency or for ecological sustainability. It was never viewed as a quick fix for environmental policy, nor was it purely a knee-jerk congressional reaction to the burgeoning environmental lobby of the late 1960s. NEPA is, in fact, a well-articulated, concise, consistent, and flexible statute that, if fully supported by the president, could be a foundation for global sustainability. Since environmental systems do not recognize political boundaries, it is crucial to develop more and better international, cooperative programs and policies. NEPA's policy model has been adopted by a majority of U.S. states and more than eighty-three countries, an impact Nicholas C. Yost, former CEQ general counsel under President Carter, suggests makes NEPA "the most imitated U.S. law in history."[42]

There are no quick and easy solutions for executing NEPA's core human values for the nation, but as we grow into the twenty-first century, let us remember what sustains our economy, our lifestyles, our spiritual selves, and the lives of future generations. Misconstruing "environmental problems" as series of isolated crises "has been a major deterrent to a serious effort to implement NEPA."[43] Unbeknownst to many in the federal government, NEPA provides a philosophical and practical context for holistic, equitable, and efficient environmental policy.

This book has attempted to integrate a wide range of literature from multiple disciplines and sources. While we have addressed the critical attributes of NEPA's genesis and evolution throughout the courts and agencies, there is much more research needed. Of particular urgency is the question of improving NEPA's integration with other laws such as those that cover wetlands, endangered species, toxic cleanup, and air pollution. NEPA is an effective and efficient vehicle for integrating and balancing disparate issues and laws, but further research is necessary in this area.

Examining the NEPA process and the science and politics of environmental policy, one must conclude that it comes down to values and the ways decision makers prioritize those values. Even if the EIS could be made a mechanical process that kicked in when some threshold environmental level was met, would we want it to be so? The time is ripe for a reconsideration of the nexus between the planetary biosphere and humankind. Unlike any other law, NEPA provides values and a policy mechanism to treat the entire social and ecological environment as fundamental to human existence. NEPA's philosophical foundations need to be resurrected, honored, and exercised. NEPA's legacy and future are in flux, but NEPA's potential is great.

The National Environmental Policy Act of 1969

Public Law 91-190 91st Congress, S.1075,
signed by President Nixon, January 1, 1970

An Act to establish a national policy for the environment, to provide for the establishment of a Council on Environmental Quality, and for other purposes. Be it enacted by the Senate and the House of Representatives of the United States of America in Congress assembled, that this Act may be cited as the "National Environmental Policy Act of 1969."

Purpose

Sec. 2. The purposes of this Act are: To declare a national policy which will encourage productive and enjoyable harmony between man and his environment; to promote efforts which will prevent or eliminate damage to the environment and biosphere and stimulate the health and welfare of man; to enrich the understanding of the ecological systems and natural resources important to the Nation; and to establish a Council on Environmental Quality.

Title I
Declaration of National Environmental Policy

Sec. 101.

(a) The Congress, recognizing the profound impact of man's activity on the interrelations of all components of the natural environment, particularly the profound influences of population growth, high-density urbanization, industrial expansion, resource exploitation, and new and expanding technological advances and recognizing further the critical importance of restoring and maintaining environmental quality to the overall welfare and development of man, declares that it is the continuing policy of the Federal Government, in cooperation with State and local governments, and other concerned public and private organizations, to use all practicable means and measures, including financial and technical assistance, in a manner calculated to foster and promote the general welfare, to create and maintain conditions under which man and nature can exist in productive harmony, and fulfill the social, economic, and other requirements of present and future generations of Americans.

(b) In order to carry out the policy set forth in this Act, it is the continuing responsibility of the Federal Government to use all practicable means, consistent with other essential considerations of national policy, to improve and coordinate Federal plans, functions, programs, and resources, to the end that the Nation may—

(i) fulfill the responsibilities of each generation as trustee of the environment for succeeding generations;

(ii) assure for all Americans safe, healthful, productive, and esthetically and culturally pleasing surroundings;

(iii) attain the widest range of beneficial uses of the environment without degradation, risk to health or safety, or other undesirable and unintended consequences;

(iv) preserve important historic, cultural, and natural aspects of our national heritage, and maintain, wherever possible, an environment which supports diversity, and variety of individual choice;

(v) achieve a balance between population and resource use which will permit high standards of living and a wide sharing of life's amenities; and

(vi) enhance the quality of renewable resources and approach the maximum attainable recycling of depletable resources.

(c)The Congress recognizes that each person should enjoy a healthful environment and that each person has a responsibility to contribute to the preservation and enhancement of the environment.

Sec. 102. The Congress authorizes and directs that, to the fullest extent possible:

(1) the policies, regulations, and public laws of the United States shall be interpreted and administered in accordance with the policies set forth in this Act, and (2) all agencies of the Federal Government shall—

(a) utilize a systematic, interdisciplinary approach which will insure the integrated use of the natural and social sciences and the environmental design arts in planning and in decision-making which may have an impact on man's environment;

(b) identify and develop methods and procedures, in consultation with the Council on Environmental Quality established by Title II of this Act, which will insure that presently unquantified environmental amenities and values be given appropriate consideration in decisionmaking, along with economic and technical considerations;

(c) include in every recommendation or report on proposals for legislation and other major Federal actions significantly affecting the quality of the human environment

(i) the environmental impact of the proposed action,
(ii) any adverse environmental effects which cannot be avoided should the proposal be implemented,
(iii) alternatives to the proposed action,
(iv) the relationship between local and short-term uses of man's environment and the maintenance and enhancement of long-term productivity, and
(v) any irreversible and irretrievable commitments of resources which would be involved in the proposed action should it be implemented. Prior to making any detailed statement, the responsible Fed-

eral official shall consult with and obtain the comments of any Federal agency which has jurisdiction by law or special expertise with respect to any environmental impact involved. Copies of such statements and the comments and views of the appropriate Federal, State, and local agencies which are authorized to develop and enforce environmental standards shall be made available to the President, the Council on Environmental Quality and to the public as provided by section 552 of Title 5, United States Code, and shall accompany the proposal through the existing agency review processes;

(d) study, develop, and describe appropriate alternatives to recommend courses of action in any proposal which involves unresolved conflicts concerning alternative uses of available resources;

(e) recognize the worldwide and long-range character of environmental problems and, where consistent with the foreign policy of the United States, lend appropriate support to initiatives, resolutions, and programs designed to maximize international cooperation in anticipating and preventing a decline in the quality of mankind's world environment;

(f) make available to States, counties, municipalities, institutions, and individuals advice and information useful in restoring, maintaining, and enhancing the quality of the environment;

(g) initiate and utilize ecological information in the planning and development of resource-oriented projects; and

(h) assist the Council on Environmental Quality established by Title II of this Act.

Sec. 103. All agencies of the Federal Government shall review their present statutory authority, administrative regulations, and current policies and procedures for the purpose of determining whether there are any deficiencies or inconsistencies therein which prohibit full compliance with the purposes and provisions of this Act and shall propose to the President not later than July 1, 1971, such measures as may be necessary to bring their authority and policies into conformity with the intent, purposes, and procedures set forth in this Act.

Sec. 104. Nothing in section 102 or 103 shall in any way affect the specific statutory obligations of any Federal agency (1) to comply with criteria or standards of environmental quality, (2) to coordinate or consult with any other Federal or State agency, or (3) to act or refrain from acting contingent upon the recommendations or certification of any other Federal or State agency.

Sec. 105. The policies and goals set forth in this Act are supplementary to those set forth in existing authorizations of Federal agencies.

Title II
Council on Environmental Quality

Sec. 201. The President shall transmit to the Congress annually beginning July 1, 1970, an Environmental Quality Report (hereinafter referred to as the "report") which shall set forth (1) the status and condition of the major natural, manmade, or altered environmental classes of the Nation, including, but not limited to, the air, the aquatic, including marine, estuarine, and fresh water, and the terrestrial environment, including, but not limited to, the forest, dry land, wetland, range, urban, suburban, and rural environment; (2) current and foreseeable trends in the quality, management, and utilization of such environments and the effects of those trends on the social, economic, and other requirements of the Nation; (3) the adequacy of available natural resources for fulfilling human and economic requirements of the Nation in the light of expected population pressures; (4) a review of the programs and activities (including regulatory activities) of the Federal Government, the State and local governments, and nongovernmental entities or individuals, with particular reference to their effect on the environment and on the conservation, development, and utilization of natural resources and activities, together with recommendations for legislation.

Sec. 202. There is created in the Executive Office of the President a Council on Environmental Quality (hereinafter referred to as the "Council"). The Council shall be composed of three members who shall be appointed by the President to serve at his pleasure, by and with the advice and consent of the Senate. The President shall designate one of the members of the Council to serve as Chairman. Each member shall be a person who, as a result of his training, experience, and attainments, is exceptionally well qualified to analyze and interpret environmental trends and information of all kinds; to appraise programs and activities of the Federal Government in the light of the policy set forth in Title I of this Act; to be conscious of and responsive to the scientific, economic, social esthetic, and cultural needs and interests of the Nation; and to formulate and recommend national policies to promote the improvement of the quality of the environment.

Sec. 203. The Council may employ such officers and employees as may be necessary to carry out its functions under this Act. In addition, the Council may employ and fix the compensation of such experts and consultants as may be necessary for the carrying out of its functions under this Act, in accordance with section 3109 of Title 5, United States Code (but without regard to the last sentence thereof).

Sec. 204. It shall be the duty and function of the Council—

(1) to assist and advise the President in the preparation of the Environmental Quality Report required by section 201;

(2) to gather timely and authoritative information concerning the conditions and trends in the quality of the environment both current and prospective, to analyze and interpret such information for the purpose of determining whether such conditions and trends are interfering, or are likely to interfere, with the achievement of the policy set forth in Title I of this Act, and to compile and submit to the President studies relating to such conditions and trends;

(3) to review and appraise the various programs and activities of the Federal Government in light of the policy set forth in Title I of this Act for the purpose of determining the extent to which such programs and activities are contributing to the achievement of such policy, and to make recommendations to the President with respect thereto;

(4) to develop and recommend to the President national policies to foster and promote the improvement of environmental quality to meet the conservation, social, economic, health, and other requirements and goals of the Nation;

(5) to conduct investigations, studies, surveys, research, and analyses relating to ecological systems and environmental quality;

(6) to document and define changes in the natural environment, including the plant and animal systems, and to accumulate necessary data and other information for a continuing analysis of these changes or trends and an interpretation of their underlying causes;

(7) to report at least once each year to the President on the state and condition of the environment; and

(8) to make and furnish such studies, reports thereon, and recommendations with respect to matters of policy and legislation as the President may request.

Sec. 205. In exercising its powers, functions, and duties under this Act, the Council shall—

(1) consult with the Citizens' Advisory Committee on Environmental Quality established by Executive Order numbered 11472, dated May 29, 1969, and with such representations of science, industry, agriculture, labor, conservation organizations, State and local governments, and other groups, as it deems advisable; and

(2) utilize, to the fullest extent possible, the services, facilities, and information (including statistical information) of public and private agencies and organizations, and individuals, in order that duplication of effort and expense may be avoided, thus assuring that the Council's activities will not unnecessarily overlap or conflict with similar activities authorized by law and performed by established agencies.

Sec. 206. Members of the Council shall serve full time and the Chairman of the Council shall be compensated at the rate provided for Level II of the Executive Schedule Pay Rates (5 U.S.C. 5313). The other members of the Council shall be compensated at the rate provided for Level IV of the Executive Schedule Pay Rates (5 U.S.C. 5315).

Sec. 207. The Council may accept reimbursements from any private nonprofit organization or from any department, agency, or instrumentality of the Federal Government, any State, or local government for the reasonable travel expenses incurred by an officer or employee of the Council in connection with his attendance at any conference, seminar, or similar meeting conducted for the benefit of the Council.

Sec. 208. The Council may make expenditures in support of its international activities, including expenditures for (1) international travel; (2) activities in implementation of international agreements; and (3) the support of international exchange programs in the United States and in foreign countries.

Sec. 209. There are authorized to be appropriated to carry out the provisions of this chapter [funds] not to exceed $300,000 for fiscal year 1970, $700,00 for fiscal year 1971, and $1,000,000 for each fiscal year thereafter.

APPENDIX B

A Partial List of NEPA Electronic Resources

CEQ Regulations: http://ceq.eh.doe.gov/nepa/regs/ceq/toc_ceq.htm

NEPA NET: http://ceq.eh.doe.gov/nepa/nepanet.htm

CEQ 1997 Annual Report (on information technology and NEPA):
http://ceq.eh.doe.gov/nepa/reports/1997/index.html

White House CEQ Web: http://www.whitehouse.gov/CEQ/html and
http://www.whitehouse.gov/CEQ/About.html

NOTES

Preface

1. CEQ website visited January 6, 2001 at http://www.whitehouse.gov/CEQ/About.html.

Chapter 1

1. The quote is from Michael Deland's statement, as chair of the Council of Environmental Quality, before the House Committee on Merchant Marine and Fisheries, Fisheries and Wildlife Conservation and the Environment Subcommittee, July 31, 1991. Quoted in Dinah Bear, "NEPA: Substance or Merely Process," *Forum for Applied Research and Public Policy* (summer 1993): 85.
2. Dinah Bear, "The National Environmental Quality Act: Its Origins and Evolution," *Natural Resources and the Environment* (fall 1995): 4. At the time of this publication, Ms. Bear was general counsel to the CEQ and in the notes to this article she acknowledges adaptation of material from Lynton Caldwell's paper "Implementing NEPA: A Non-Technical Political Task," written for the CEQ in 1994.
3. Daniel R. Mandelker, *NEPA Law and Litigation: The National Environmental Policy Act*, Sec. 1:01.
4. James Hansen, "Law Doesn't Accomplish Its Goals," *Roll Call*, April 19, 1999, 9–10.
5. Frank Pallone, "Thirty Years of NEPA: It Works in My State," *Roll Call*, Monday, April 19, 1999, 9.
6. Lynton K. Caldwell, "NEPA Revisited: A Call for a Constitutional Amendment," *Environmental Forum* (November–December 1989): 19.
7. Zygmunt J. B. Plater, Robert H. Abrams, and William Goldfarb, *Environmental Law and Policy: Nature, Law, and Society*, 598.
8. As cited in Lynton K. Caldwell, *A National Environmental Policy Act*, 123.
9. Frederick R. Anderson assisted by Robert H. Daniels, *NEPA in the Courts: A Legal Analysis of the National Environmental Policy Act*.
10. Lynton Caldwell, "The Ecosystem as a Criterion for Public Land Policy," *Natu-*

ral Resources Journal 10 (2): 220. Caldwell was addressing the early congressional attempts to legislate environmental conditions and problems. The first federal "environmental policies" were developed in the early twentieth century. Although we trace major contemporary federal environmental policies to the Clean Air Act of 1955, earlier laws also dealt with the environment. Many of these laws, including the establishment of national forests, were developed from a utilitarian view of resources and a mechanistic view of environment. It can also be argued that these were written not to preserve or protect the environment but to further commerce—often at the expense of the environment. For example, the 1899 Rivers and Harbors Act, although subsequently used as a measure to combat water pollution, was originally designed to insure the safe movement of interstate commerce.

11. James McElfish and Elissa Parker, *Rediscovering the National Environmental Policy Act: Back to the Future*, 11.

12. Senate Committee on Interior and Insular Affairs, Hearings on S. 1075, S. 237, and S. 1752, 92d Congress, 1st sess., April 16, 1969, pp. 116–17.

13. Lynton K. Caldwell, *A National Environmental Policy Act*, 48.

14. Lynton K. Caldwell, "Environment: A New Focus for Public Policy?" *Public Administration Review* 23 (1963): 132. Rachel Carson, *Silent Spring;* Stewart Udall, *The Quiet Crisis;* and Barry Commoner, *The Closing Circle.*

15. National Environmental Policy Act of 1969, 42 U.S.C. 4321.

16. Lettie M. Wenner, *The Environmental Decade in Court;* also Frederick R. Anderson, Daniel R. Mandelker, and A. Don Tarlock, *Environmental Protection: Law and Policy.* See also two bibliographies that cover roughly the first decade of NEPA: Robert Lazear, *The National Environmental Policy Act and Its Implementation: A Selected, Annotated Bibliography;* and John P. Worsham, *The National Environmental Policy Act and Related Matters: A Selected Bibliography.*

17. Serge Taylor, *Making Bureaucracies Think: The Environmental Impact Strategy of Administrative Reform.*

18. Daniel A. Dreyfus and Helen M. Ingram, "The National Environmental Policy Act: A View of Intent and Practice," *Natural Resources Journal* 16 (2): 246. Taylor cited in Robert V. Bartlett, "Rationality and the Logic of the National Environmental Policy Act," *Environmental Professional* 8 (1986): 105–11.

19. Lynton K. Caldwell, "Beyond NEPA: Future Significance of the National Environmental Policy Act," *Harvard Environmental Law Review* 22, no. 2032, 203.

20. Personal communication with Lynton Caldwell (Sept. 8, 1994).

21. Zygmunt J. B. Plater, Robert H. Abrams, and William Goldfarb, *Environmental Law and Policy: Nature, Law, and Society*, 598.

22. We put major federal action in quotation marks because what constitutes a federal action has been subject to widespread debate and interpretation throughout the various NEPA court decisions. The CEQ regulations define major federal actions as: "actions with effects that may be major and which are potentially subject to Federal control and responsibility. Actions include

new and continuing activities, including projects and programs entirely or partly financed, assisted, conducted, regulated, or approved by federal agencies; new or revised agency rules, regulations, plans, policies, or procedures; and legislative proposals. Actions do not include funding assistance solely in the form of general revenue-sharing funds, distributed under the State and Local Fiscal Assistance Act of 1972, 31 U.S.C. 1221 et seq., with no Federal agency control over subsequent use of such funds. Actions do not include bringing judicial or administrative civil or criminal enforcement actions."

23. F. Anderson, *NEPA in the Courts;* Dreyfus and Ingram, "The National Environmental Policy Act," 243–62; Richard Liroff, *A National Policy for the Environment;* Walter Rosenbaum, "The End of Illusion: NEPA and the Limits of Judicial Review," in *Environmental Politics;* and Geoffrey Wandesforde-Smith et al., "Policy Impact Analysis and Environmental Management: Review and Comment," *Policy Studies Journal* 4 (1): 81–90.

Chapter 2

1. James E. Anderson, *Public Policy-Making,* 85. See also Randall Ripley and Grace A. Franklin, *Policy Implementation and Bureaucracy,* 45, 54.
2. Caldwell, "Beyond NEPA," 203.
3. Kingdon, 1984, provides a well-informed model for policy development that further examines the notion of policy windows of opportunity and related concepts.
4. See especially Richard N. L. Andrews and Serge Taylor, "Making Bureaucracies Think," in *Making Bureaucracies Think: The Environmental Impact Strategy of Administrative Reform.*
5. Aldo Leopold, *A Sand County Almanac.*
6. Samuel P. Hays, *Beauty, Health, and Permanence: Environmental Politics in the United States, 1955–1985,* 3; Ronald Inglehart, *The Silent Revolution: Changing Values and Political Styles among Western Publics.*
7. It should be noted that the Ehrlichs' work has endured some sharp criticism from other scholars, such as Julian L. Simon, *The Ultimate Resource,* and a more recent book by Michael Sanera and Jane Shaw, *Facts, Not Fear: A Parent's Guide to Teaching Children about the Environment.* Both critics contend that the Ehrlichs are part of a "gloom and doom" politicized environmental movement that disregards factual information to further justify regulations that limit individual liberty. For more information about Garrett Hardin, see "The Tragedy of the Commons," *Science,* 162 (1968): 1243–48.
8. John C. Whitaker, *Striking a Balance: Environment and Natural Resources Policy in the Nixon–Ford Years,* 264.
9. David Vogel, *National Styles of Regulation: Environmental Policy in Great Britain*

    and the United States, 20. For more information on the growth of environmental groups see also Riley E. Dunlap and Angela G. Mertig, eds., *American Environmentalism: The U.S. Environmental Movement 1970–1990.*

10. Wenner, *The Environmental Decade in Court.*

11. Caldwell, "Environment: A New Focus," 134. A revised version is reprinted as chapter 1 in Caldwell's *Environment: A Challenge to Modern Society,* 20. See also Caldwell, "Restructuring for Coordinative Policy and Action," *Public Administration Review* 28 (1968): 301–303.

12. Caldwell, "Environment: A New Focus," 136; Caldwell, *Environment: A Challenge to Modern Society,* 20, 136.

13. The mutually accommodating relationship between interest groups, bureaucrats, and legislative committee members is described as an "iron triangle." These political actors become entangled in the mutual pursuit of more federal dollars for favored programs and offices. For a general discussion, see Randall Ripley and Grace A. Franklin, *Congress, the Bureaucracy, and Public Policy.* For a thorough analysis of how iron triangles and "issue networks" are politically malleable and subject to outside influence, see Daniel McCool's *Command of the Waters: Iron Triangles, Federal Water Development, and Indian Water.*

14. Caldwell, "Environment: A New Focus," 137, 138.

15. As cited in Lynton K. Caldwell, *A National Environmental Policy Act,* 60–61.

16. Caldwell with Van Ness, *A National Policy for the Environment,* 19.

17. Caldwell, "Environment: A New Focus," 138.

18. Charles Lindblom, *The Intelligence of Democracy;* Lindblom, *The Policy-Making Process;* Lindblom, "The Science of 'Muddling Through,'" *Public Administration Review* 19 (spring 1959): 79–88.

19. René Dubos wrote about First-World complacency in the face of environmental catastrophe in his 1968 essay, "Man and His Environment: Adaptations and Interactions," in *The Fitness of Man's Environment, Smithsonian Annual 2,* and in *Reason Awake: Science for Man.* Dubos basically contends that certain societies gradually adapt to progressively worsening ecological conditions. But these societies are only ones in which "populations have not outrun adequate supplies of uncontaminated food and water, and in which concentrations of populations are not so large as to be totally dependent upon the uninterrupted functioning of mechanized supply systems"; cited in Lynton Caldwell, "Environmental Policy in a Hypertrophic Society," *Natural Resources Journal* 11 (July 1971): 420. "Crisis" decision making is a widely discussed topic. See, for example, Graham Allison's *Essence of Decision: Explaining the Cuban Missile Crisis,* and Zachary A. Smith's *Environmental Policy Paradox.*

20. Jackson testimony, Senate Committee on Interior and Insular Affairs, 90th Cong., 2d Sess.; cited in Caldwell with Van Ness, *A National Policy for the Environment,* Senate Committee on Interior and Insular Affairs, Hearings on S. 1075, p. 30.

21. Caldwell, "NEPA Revisited," 18.

22. Zygmunt J. B. Plater, Robert H. Abrams, and Williams Goldfarb, *Environmental Law and Policy: Nature, Law, and Society,* 603.

23. Senate Committee on Interior and Insular Affairs, *National Environmental Policy Act of 1969,* Conference Report, *Congressional Record,* vol. 115, part 30, 91st Cong., 1st sess., p. 40416.

24. Quoted in Caldwell, *Environment: A Challenge to Modern Society,* 172.

25. Caldwell, *Environment: A Challenge to Modern Society,* 191–212.

26. The Multiple Use–Sustained Yield Act of 1960 (16 U.S.C.A., secs. 528 and 531) is an example of a land management policy applied to specific federal lands—in this instance the U.S. Forest Service. Although "multiple-use" purports to manage lands with many different goals in mind, attention to the interrelationship of the resources themselves has never been a Forest Service priority.

27. Caldwell, "NEPA Revisited," 18.

28. House Committee on Science and Astronautics, Subcommittee on Science, Research, and Development, *Managing the Environment,* 90th Congress, 2d sess., 1969, Committee Print.

29. House-Senate Joint Colloquium to Discuss a National Policy for the Environment, 90th Congress, 2d sess., 1968, 1–2.

30. *Congressional White Paper on a National Policy for the Environment,* special report to the U.S. Senate Committee on Interior and Insular Affairs, 1–2.

31. Ibid., 1–2.

32. Ibid., 17.

33. House-Senate Joint Colloquium, 6.

34. See, for example, USALSA Report: Environmental Law Division, "Note: Fourth Circuit Court Looks at NEPA Cost Benefit Analysis," *Army Lawyer* 38, June, 1999.

35. House-Senate Joint Colloquium, 39.

36. Cited in *Congressional White Paper on a National Policy for the Environment,* 4. Although NEPA did not directly address Caldwell's proposal, it is still very relevant today considering that we have been experiencing unprecedentedly cheap energy (using inflation-adjusted prices) and that environmental externalities (costs not included in price of product and costs shifted to the public or some third party) are often inadequately addressed either as a cost or a benefit. Primarily, this is because ecological, aesthetic, and spiritual values attached to the human and nonhuman world are often difficult to quantify, test, and evaluate in monetary terms. For example, if ecological scarcity was computed within a benefit-cost decision-making structure, it would make sense economically (not just aesthetically) to move to renewable energy sources and conservationist public policies because these would cost less money.

37. *Congressional White Paper on a National Policy for the Environment,* 18.

38. Ibid., 16.

Chapter 3

1. Geoffrey Wandesforde-Smith, "National Policy for the Environment: Politics and the Concept of Stewardship," in *Congress and the Environment*, 208.

2. Senate Committee on Interior and Insular Affairs, Hearings on S. 1075, S. 237, and S. 1752, 83.

3. A key historical difference between the Employment Act and NEPA is the context in which these two pieces of legislation were constructed. In 1946 the ideas surrounding the maintenance of an already steady pattern of economic growth unsurprisingly enjoyed strong public support. In the late 1960s public concern for environmental preservation had undoubtedly grown from years past but still commanded no more than 50 percent of the public's interest.

4. *Congressional White Paper on a National Policy for the Environment*, 104.

5. Ibid.

6. Congress cannot constitutionally delegate legislative authority to an executive agency. Whether President Nixon was more concerned with the constitutional separation of powers issue or with preventing the creation of an independent agency is an open question.

7. Senate Committee on Interior and Insular Affairs, Hearings on S. 1075, pp. 3–14.

8. For a detailed description of the various federal agencies with responsibilities for the environment, see appendix C in Caldwell with Van Ness, *A National Policy for the Environment*, 124–26.

9. Senate Committee on Interior and Insular Affairs, Hearings on S. 1075, p. 177.

10. *Congressional Record*, 91st Congress, 1st sess., 1969, vol. 115, pt. 11, p. 14861.

11. Senate Committee on Interior and Insular Affairs, Hearings on S. 1075, S. 237, and S. 1752.

12. Sec. 103, NEPA.

13. Nicholas Yost, "NEPA's Promise—Partially Fulfilled," *Environmental Law* 20 (1990): 536; Richard N. L. Andrews, *Environmental Policy and Administrative Change: Implementation of the National Environmental Policy Act*, 17; Lynton Caldwell, *Science and the National Environmental Policy Act: Redirecting Policy through Procedural Reform*.

14. Statement by Daniel Dreyfus, cited in Liroff, *NEPA and Its Aftermath;* Senate Committee on Interior and Insular Affairs, "National Environmental Policy Act of 1969," 24.

15. Senate Committee on Interior and Insular Affairs, "National Environmental Policy Act of 1969."

16. See U.S. Senate, *National Environmental Policy Act of 1969*, 1–4; see also *Congressional Record*, vol. 115, 19008, 19013.

17. Cited in Liroff, *A National Policy*, 23.

18. Liroff, *A National Policy*, 33.

19. *Congressional Record,* vol. 115, 26589.
20. The following are congressional bills that proposed some sort of statutory environmental council.

    S. 1075 (Jackson) Three-member board of environmental-quality advisers. Passed Senate July 10, 1969.

    S. 237 (McGovern) Three-member council on environmental quality.

    S. 1085 (Nelson) Five-member council on environmental quality.

    H.R. 25, 6750 (Dingell) Three-member council on environmental quality.

    H.R. 12549 9 (Dingell) Five-member council (Revision of H.R. 6750).

    H.R. 3329 (Tunney) Nine-member council of ecological advisers.

    H.R. 7016 (Moss) Five-2member national council on the environment.

    Other bills included H.R. 6955 (Corman), H.R. 79232 (Howard), H.R. 8806 (Podell), H.R. 8588 (Ashley), H.R. 11937 (Foley), H.R. 11942 (Griffiths), etc.

    See also *Environmental Quality: Selected Bills and Resolutions,* compiled by Maureen W. Ayton. Washington, D.C.: Library of Congress Legislative Reference Service, Science Policy Research Division, June 20, 1969, 8.
21. *Congressional Quarterly Almanac,* 525.
22. For more discussion on the phenomenon of "groupthink," see Allison's *Essence of Decision,* and Irving Janis's *Victims of Groupthink: A Psychological Study of Foreign-Policy Decisions and Fiascoes.*
23. As cited in Liroff, *A National Policy,* 22.
24. *Congressional Quarterly Almanac,* 513.
25. The interagency committee is discussed in *Congressional Record,* vol. 115, 29061.
26. Ibid., 26590.
27. Liroff, *A National Policy,* 34.
28. There was some talk of giving the CEQ "stop-order" authority if it deemed a project or decision unfit for any number of reasons. This veto power was eventually put on hold primarily for two reasons. First, this was a controversial measure and the Dingell subcommittee wanted to insure the bill's passage, and second, the Dingell bill was molded after the Full Employment Act and this precedent lacked any "stop-order" authority.
29. *Congressional Quarterly Almanac,* 513.
30. Dreyfus and Ingram, "The National Environmental Policy Act," 251. Some members of Congress thought the president was simply trying to steal the political fire generated by Congressional action on this issue, especially since environmental concerns were becoming politically salient, and the 1972

presidential race was quickly approaching, with former senator Edward Muskie, an environmentalist, the Democratic front-runner. Political jockeying for the "environmental card" was, of course, also going on among the Democrats.

31. Senate Committee on Interior and Insular Affairs, Hearings on S.1075, 73–74.
32. Ibid., 119.
33. Personal communication, Lynton Caldwell, September 8, 1994.
34. Senate Committee on Interior and Insular Affairs, Hearings on S.1075, p. 124.
35. *Congressional Record,* vol. 115, 15544.
36. Ibid., 29053.
37. See ibid., 29051, for the full text.
38. Cited in Timothy O'Riordan, *Environmentalism,* 284.
39. Prior to this change, Jackson's bill somewhat arrogantly required the executive environmental report be distributed only to Jackson's Interior and Insular Affairs Committee. *Congressional Record,* vol. 115, pt. 21, 29061.
40. *Congressional Record,* vol. 39, pt. 702, 40417–18 (Senate Report no. 91-296).
41. For additional discussion on this, see the "Statement of Managers on the Part of the House" as appended to the conference report and reprinted in *Congressional Record,* vol. 115, 39702.
42. For the full text see *Congressional Record,* vol. 115, 29051.
43. Roger W. Findley and Daniel Farber, *Environmental Law in a Nutshell,* 21.
44. *Congressional Quarterly Almanac,* 527.
45. Cited in Dreyfus and Ingram, "The National Environmental Policy Act," 251.
46. Dreyfus and Ingram, "The National Environmental Policy Act," 252; *Congressional Record,* vol. 115, 39703. In one of the Supreme Court's few environmentally favorable NEPA decisions, this legislative history was also recognized by the Court in *Flint Ridge Dev. Co. v. Scenic Rivers Ass'n* (1976).
47. *Congressional Record,* vol. 115, 40923–28, 40415–27.
48. "Nixon Promises an Urgent Fight to End Pollution," *New York Times,* January 2, 1970, Sec. A, 1.
49. *Public Papers of the President, Richard M. Nixon,* 2.
50. This is intrinsically neither good nor bad, rather it is a natural phenomenon of an institution that revolves around established political precedent and constraints—including the constant pressure of reelection.
51. Cited in Dreyfus and Ingram, "The National Environmental Policy Act," 243.
52. Lynton Caldwell noted that even after twenty-five years most national environmental organizations have not fully understood, much less fully utilized, the potential power and importance of NEPA (personal communication, October 15, 1995).
53. *Congressional Record,* vol. 115, 40416; see Nicholas Yost, "NEPA's Promise— Partially Fulfilled," *Environmental Law* 20 (1990): 534.
54. Dreyfus and Ingram, "The National Environmental Policy Act," 243.

Chapter 4

1. Quoted in Kenneth R. Hammond, ed., *Judgment and Decision in Public Policy Formation*, 5.
2. There is a presumption of objectivity in science that may or may not be accurate. Some have argued that the values science pursues color and lead to conclusions that, if not preordained, are at least not value-free. See, for example, Hilary Rose and Steven Rose, eds., *The Political Economy of Science.*
3. Paul J. Culhane and Paul H. Friesema, "Social Impacts, Politics, and the Environmental Impact Statement," *Natural Resources Journal* 16 (1976): 340–41.
4. Douglas Amy, "Decision Techniques for Environmental Policy," in *Managing Leviathan: Environmental Politics and the Administrative State,* 59–79.
5. Wade L. Robison, *Decisions in Doubt: The Environment and Public Policy,* 3.
6. Paul Feyerabend, *Science in a Free Society,* 88.
7. Paul R. Ehrlich and Anne H. Ehrlich, *Betrayal of Science and Reason: How Anti-Environmental Rhetoric Threatens Our Future.*
8. See Hilary Rose and Steven Rose, eds., *The Radicalisation of Science.*
9. Brian Martin, "Anarchist Science Policy," *Raven* 7, no. 2 (summer, 1994): 140–41.
10. Bear, "NEPA: Substance or Merely Process?" 85–88.
11. U.S. Senate, *National Environmental Policy Act of 1969,* pt. 14.
12. Title I, Sec. 101 (b).
13. Purpose, Sec. 2.
14. 42 U.S.C., Sec. 101 (a) Sec. 4331.
15. For more on ecological rationality see works by Robert V. Bartlett, "Ecological Rationality: Reason and Environmental Policy." *Environmental Ethics,* 221–39.
16. Council on Environmental Quality, *The National Environmental Policy Act: A Study of Its Effectiveness after Twenty-Five Years,* iii.
17. Senate Committee on Interior and Insular Affairs, Hearings on S. 1075, 116.
18. Quoted in Dreyfus and Ingram, "The National Environmental Policy Act," 246.
19. Amy, "Decision Techniques for Environmental Policy," 60.
20. *Congressional Record,* vol. 115, 5820.
21. 42 U.S.C., Sec. 102, Sec. 4332 (1988).
22. 42 U.S.C. Sec. 102, (2) (A) Sec. 4332 (1988).
23. Ibid.
24. Ibid., Sec. 102 (2) (C) (i)–(v), Sec. 4321 et seq.
25. Sec. 102 (2) (G) requires federal agencies to "initiate and utilize ecological information in the planning and development of resource orientated projects."
26. Lynton Caldwell and Robert Bartlett led a thorough review of NEPA in a National Science Foundation–funded study, *A Study of Ways to Improve the Scientific Content and Methodology of Environmental Impact Analysis.* See also Lynton Caldwell, "Understanding Impact Analysis: Technical Process, Administrative

Reform, Policy Principle," in *Policy through Impact Assessment: Institutional Analysis as a Policy Strategy.*

27. Julian Dunster, "Assessing the Sustainability of Canadian Forest Management: Progress or Procrastination?" *Environmental Impact Assessment Review* 12 (1992): 67–84; Robert Bartlett, "Ecological Reason in Administration: Environmental Impact Assessment and Administrative Theory," in *Managing Leviathan: Environmental Politics and the Administrative State.*

28. Paul J. Culhane, H. Paul Friesema, and Janice A. Beecher, *Forecasts and Environmental Decisionmaking: The Content and Predictive Accuracy of Environmental Impact Statements.*

29. 42 U.S.C. Sec. 102, Sec. 4332 (1) (1988).

30. U.S. Senate, *National Environmental Policy Act of 1969*, pt. 14, at 19.

31. Hanna Cortner, "A Case Analysis of Policy Implementation: The National Environmental Policy Act of 1969," *Natural Resources Journal* 16 (1976): 323–38.

Chapter 5

1. Valerie M. Fogleman, *Guide to the National Environmental Policy Act: Interpretations, Applications, and Compliance*, 30.

2. Executive Order No. 11514 required the CEQ to issue EIS guidelines. See Executive Order 11514, 35 *Federal Register* 4247 (1970) and Executive Order No. 11991, 42 *Federal Register* 26, 967 (1977).

3. As cited in Clay Hartman, "NEPA: Business as Usual: The Weaknesses of the National Environmental Policy Act," 717.

4. 43 *Federal Register* 55994, November 29, 1978, Sec. 1502.1.

5. Accessed in January 6, 2001 at http://www.whitehouse.gov/CEQ/About.html

6. C.F.R., 40 Sec. 1500.1–28, (1989) and "Worst Case Analysis: A Continued Requirement under the National Environmental Policy Act?" *Columbia Journal of Environmental Law* 53 (1987): 60.

7. C.F.R., 40 Sec. 15022.22 (1986).

8. U.S. Senate, *National Environmental Policy Act of 1969*, pt. 14.

9. Senate Committee on Interior and Insular Affairs, Hearings on S. 1075, S. 237, and S. 1752, 116–17, 121.

10. These actions were included in the CEQ's "interim guidelines" for preparing EISs. The CEQ stated that NEPA applied, but was not limited to, the following actions:

> (i) Recommendations or reports relating to legislation and appropriations.
> (ii) Projects and continuing activities;
>   -Directly undertaken by Federal Agencies;
>   -Supported in whole or in part through Federal contracts,

grants, subsidies, loans, or other forms of funding assistance;
-Policy and procedure making.
35 *Federal Register* 7390 (May 12, 1970).

11. Council on Environmental Quality, Annual Report 1994.
12. Office of Environmental Quality Authorization, Fiscal Years 1989–1993; House Committee on Merchant Marine and Fisheries, Subcommittee on Fisheries and Wildlife Conservation and the Environment, Hearings on H.R. 1113, pp. 59–60 (statement of Jennifer Wilson, assistant administrator for external affairs, EPA).
13. Derived from NEPA and EPA regualtions as reported in Alan Gilpin, *Environmental Impact Assessment (EIA): Cutting Edge for the Twenty-First Century* (Cambridge: Cambridge University Press, 1995).
14. 40 C.F.R. Sec. 1508.28 (1993).
15. 40 C.F.R. Sec. 1508.14 (1993).
16. David B. Firestone and Frank C. Reed, *Environmental Law for Non-Lawyers*, 3; see also 40 C.F.R. Sec. 1508.27.
17. National Environmental Policy Act of 1969, Sec. 101.
18. See C.F.R., Title 40, chap. 5, Sec. 1508.4 for the CEQ's discussion of "categorical exclusions" or "a category of actions which do not individually or cumulatively have a significant effect on the human environment."
19. See William A. Tilleman, "Public Participation in Environmental Impact Assessment Process: A Comparative Study of Impact Assessment in Canada, the United States, and the European Community," *Columbia Journal of Transnational Law* (1995): 337, from which most of the international comparative material in this case study was taken.
20. Ibid.
21. Besides the *Code of Federal Regulations*, see also Nicholas C. Yost, "Scoping Guidance." Also helpful in many ways is Yost, "Forty Most Asked Questions Concerning CEQ's National Environmental Policy Act Regulations," reprinted in the *Federal Register* 46, no. 18026 (March 23, 1981), as amended.
22. 40 C.F.R. Sec. 1508.25 (1993).
23. Material on the Portsmouth, Virginia, oil refinery case is taken from Richard A. Liroff, "Oil vs. Oysters—Lessons for Environmental Regulation of Industrial Siting from the Hampton Roads Refinery Controversy," *Boston College Environmental Affairs Law Review* 11 (fall 1984): 705.
24. *Scientists' Institute for Public Information, Inc. v. AEC*, 481 F. 2d 1079 (D.C. Cir. 1973).
25. Council on Environmental Quality, 1996 Annual Report, 13.
26. 40 C.F.R. Sec. 1508.7.
27. CEQ Annual Report, 1997, p. 15.
28. 5 U.S.C. Sec. 706 (2)(A).
29. 40 C.F.R. Sec. 1502.14.

30. 40 C.F.R. Sec. 1501.1 (1993).

31. Council on Environmental Quality, *The National Environmental Policy Act: A Study of Its Effectiveness after Twenty-Five Years.*

32. *Scientist's Institute for Public Information (SIPI) v. Atomic Energy Commission,* 1086–87, 1095.

33. 40 C.F.R. Sec. 1508.23 (1993).

34. Zygmunt J.B. Plater, Robert H. Abrams, and William Goldfarb, *Environmental Law and Policy: Nature, Law, and Society,* 638.

35. Liroff, *A National Policy,* 88.

36. The information about the pipeline case study comes from *Wilderness Society v. Morton,* 463 F. 2d 1261 (D.C. Cir. 1972).

37. Liroff, *A National Policy,* 89.

38. CEQ Regulations, Sec. 1501.6., 43 *Federal Register* 55990, November 28, 1978

39. Environmental Protection Agency, Office of Federal Activities, "Policy and Procedures for the Review of Federal Actions Impacting the Environment," October 3, 1984, available at http://es.epa.gov/oeca/ofa/84policy.html, December 6, 1999.

40. Kelly Tzoumis and Linda Finegold, "Looking at the Quality of Draft Environmental Impact Statements in the United States over Time: Have Ratings Improved?" typescript, 1999.

41. Ibid., 12.

42. Council on Environmental Quality, *The National Environmental Policy Act,* 17.

43. E.P.A., Office of Federal Activities, "EIS Page Lenghths," accessed on January 2, 2001 at http://es.epa.gov/oeca/ofa/length.html.

44. Council on Environmental Quality, *The National Environmental Policy Act,* 17.

45. Lynton K. Caldwell, *A National Envoronmental Policy Act,* 101.

46. Council on Environmental Quality, Executive Office of the President, memorandum to Heads of Agencies on the Application of the National Environmental Policy Act to Proposed Federal Actions in the United States with Transboundary Effects, July 1, 1997. Available at http://ceq.eh.doe.gov/nepa/regs/transguide.html. Accessed on Jan. 8, 2001.

47. Caldwell, *National Environmental Policy Act,* 106.

48. Quoted in Paul S. Weiland, "Amending the National Environmental Policy Act: Federal Environmental Protection in the Twenty-First Century," *Journal of Land Use and Environmental Law* 12 (spring 1997): 275.

49. Andrews, *Environmental Policy and Administrative Change,* xvi.

50. 449 F. 2d 1109 (D.C. Cir. 1971), cert. denied, 404 U.S. 942 (1972).

51. Robert F. Blomquist, "Supplemental Environmental Impact Statements under NEPA: A Conceptual Synthesis and Critique of Existing Legal Approaches to Environmental and Technological Changes," *Temple Environmental Law and Technology Journal* 8 (fall 1989): 3.

52. Dinah Bear, "The National Environmental Policy Act," *Intergovernmental Perspective* (summer 1992): 18.

53. Robert Davis, "Do We Exalt EIS Form over Substance?" in *Environmental Impact Assessment: Proceedings of a Conference on the Preparation and Review of Environmental Impact Statements*, 203.

54. Council on Environmental Quality, *Environmental Quality: Twenty-Second Annual Report*, March 1992, 135.

Chapter 6

1. Fogleman, *Guide to the National Environmental Policy Act.*

2. Plater, Abrams, and Goldfarb, *Environmental Law and Policy: Nature, Law, and Society*, 603.

3. *Chevron, U.S.A., Inc. v. Natural Resources Defense Council*, 467 U.S. 837. 104 S. Ct. 2778, 81 L. Ed. 2d 694.

4. *Stryker's Bay Neighborhood Council v. Karlen*, 100 S. Ct. 497 (1980); *Aberdeen & Rockfish R.R. v. Students Challenging Agency Regulatory Procedures*, 422 U.S. 289 (1975) (SCRAP II); *Vermont Yankee Nuclear Power Co. v. Natural Resources Defense Council*, 435 U.S. 519, 98 S. Ct. 1197, 55 L. Ed. 2d (1978); *Robertson v. Methow Valley Citizens Council*, 109 S. Ct. 1835 (1989).

5. 449 F. 2d 1109 (1971).

6. Courts have held similar findings in the following cases; *Sierra Club v. Morton*, 405 U.S. 727 (1972); *United States v. Students Challenging Regulatory Agency Procedures*, 412 U.S. 669 (1973) (SCRAP I); *Warm Springs Dam Task Force v. Gribble*, 565 F.2d 549, 9th Cir. (1977).

7. For analyses of the historical aspects of standing, see Raoul Berger, "Standing to Sue in Public Actions: Is It a Constitutional Requirement?" *Yale Law Journal* 78 (1969): 816; Louis L. Jaffe, "Standing to Secure Judicial Review: Public Actions," *Harvard Law Review* 74 (1961): 1265–1314; Jaffe, "Standing to Secure Judicial Review: Private Actions," *Harvard Law Review* 75 (1961): 255; Lee A. Albert, "Standing to Challenge Administrative Action: An Inadequate Surrogate for Claim for Relief," *Yale Law Journal* 83 (1974): 425–27 (describes development of standing controversies in the 1920s and 1930s); William A. Fletcher, "The Structure of Standing," *Yale Law Journal* 98 (1988): 221–91 (genesis of standing law in the 1930s).

8. U.S. Constitution, art. 3, Sec. 2, cl. 1. *Allen v. Wright*, 468 U.S. 737, 770 (1984); Brennan's dissent was in part a quote from *Baker v. Carr*, 369 U.S. 186, 204 (1962).

9. *Duke Power Co. v. Carolina Environmental Study Group, Inc.*, 438 U.S. 59, 73–74 (1978); *Sierra Club v. Morton*, 733–38.

10. *Simon v. Eastern Ky. Welfare Rights Org.*, 426 U.S. 26, 41–42, 38 (1976).

11. *Valley Forge Christian College v. Americans United for Separation of Church and State, Inc.*, 454 U.S. 464, 471 (1982).

12. *Warth v. Seldin*, 422 U.S. 490, 499 (1975).

13. This test comes primarily from the Administrative Procedure Act (APA) rather than a broad prudential requirement. See also *Association of Data Processing Service Organizations, Inc. v. Camp,* 397 U.S. 150, 153 (1970), discussed below.

14. While NEPA does not contain a "citizen suit provision," largely because it was enacted before Congress used this more regularly, several more recent important environmental laws do contain this provision. Among the major environmental acts that authorize citizen suits enforcement are the Endangered Species Act Sec. 11(g), 16 U.S.C. Sec. 1540 (g) (1988); Surface Mining and Control Act and Reclamation Act Sec. 520, 30 U.S.C. Sec. 1270 (1988); Toxic Substances Control Act Sec. 20, 15 U.S.C. Sec. 2619 (1988); and Clean Water Act Sec. 505, 33 U.S.C. Sec. 1365 (1988).

15. 5 U.S.C. Sec. 702 (1988).

16. 397 U.S. 150 (1970).

17. *Sierra Club v. Morton,* 739.

18. Ibid., 734–35.

19. *SCRAP I,* 412 U.S. 669 (1973).

20. Ibid., 679.

21. Ibid., 688.

22. 110 S. Ct. 3177, 3182, 3184 (1990).

23. Ibid., 3189.

24. 110 S. Ct. 3185, 3189–91.

25. 112 S. Ct. 2130 (1992).

26. *Lujan v. Defenders,* 2130 (1992).

27. Cases are, respectively, *City of Rochester v. United States Postal Service,* 541 F. 2d 967, 972 (2d. Cir. 1976); *Pennsylvania v. Morton,* 381 F. Supp. 293, 300 (D.D.C. 1974); *National Helium Corp. v. Morton,* 455 F. 2d 650, 655 (10th Cir. 1971); *Port of Astoria v. Hodel,* 595 F. 2d 950, 951 (3d. Cir. 1976); *Lake Erie Alliance for Protection of Coastal Corridor v. Corps of Engineers,* 486 F. Supp. 707, 710–14 (W.D. Pa. 1980).

28. *Baltimore Gas and Electric Co. v. Natural Resources Defense Council, Inc.,* 462 U.S. 87, 97 (1983).

29. 42 U.S.C. 4332; 40 C.F.R. 1502.3.

30. Firestone and Reed, *Environmental Law for Non-Lawyers,* 30. Cases are, respectively, *Save Our Ten Acres v. Kreger,* 472 F. 2d 463, 467 (1973); *Minnesota Public Interest Research Group (MPIRG) v. Butz,* 498 F.2d 1314, 1320 (1974); *SCRAP v. U.S.,* 346 F. Supp. 189, 201 (1972); and finally, *Hanly v. Kleindienst,* 471 F. 2d 823, 831 (1972).

31. 42 U.S.C. Sec. 4332 (2) (C) (1988).

32. *NAACP v. Medical Center, Inc.* 584 F. 2d 619, 626–27, 634 (3d. Cir. 1978); *Hanly v. Mitchell,* 460 F. 2d 640 (2d Cir.) cert. denied, 409 U.S. 990 (1972).

33. *Sierra Club v. Hodel,* 848 F. 2d 661, 673 n. 15 (9th Cir. 1975); *MPIRG,* 1321–22.

34. *City of Davis v. Coleman,* 521 F. 2d 551, 673 n. 15 (9th Cir. 1975).

35. *MPIRG,* 1314.

36. 498 F. 2d 1321 8th Cir. (1974).

37. 471 F. 2d 823 (2d Cir. 1972), cert. denied, 412 U.S. 908 (1973).
38. Ibid., 830–31.
39. 460 U.S. 766 (1983).
40. Administrative Procedures Act, 5 U.S.C.A. Sec. 701.
41. 309 F. Supp. 1189 (W.D. Tenn.), 432 F. 2d 1307, 1 ELR 20053 (6th Cir. 1970), reviewed, 401 U.S. 402, 1 ELR 20110 (U.S. 1971).
42. Findley and Farber, *Environmental Law in a Nutshell*, 16–17.
43. As cited in Plater, Adams, and Goldfarb, *Environmental Law and Policy*, 635.
44. *Overton Park*, 416.
45. *Calvert Cliffs'*, 1111.
46. Ibid., 1112, 1114, 1109.
47. 449 F. 2d 1109 (D.C. Cir. 1971).
48. *Kleppe v. Sierra Club*, 427 U.S. 390 (1976), 421.
49. Ibid., 390, 410.
50. *Vermont Yankee*, 460 (1978). Clearly, justices and judges have no place deciding the appropriate method of analysis within a technical field such as physics, forestry, chemistry or the like. However, courts must uphold our laws even when unpopular with the public or federal agencies.
51. Ibid., 544.
52. Ibid., 558.
53. Ibid., 548.
54. Ibid., 547.
55. 444 U.S., 227–28 (quoting *Kleppe v. Sierra Club*, 410 n. 21).
56. *Marsh v. Oregon Natural Resources Council*, 109 S. Ct. (1989), 1851.
57. David C. Shilton, "Is the Supreme Court Hostile to NEPA? Some Possible Explanations for a 12–0 record," *Environmental Law* 20 (1990): 551–68; Goldsmith and Banks, "Environmental Values: Institutional Responsibility and the Supreme Court," *Harvard Environmental Law Review* 7 (1983): 5–6.
58. *Environmental Law for Non-Lawyers*, 31.
59. *American Public Transit Association v. Goldschmidt*, 485 F. Supp. 991 (1992).
60. *Goose Hollow Foothills League v. Romney*, 334 F. Supp. 877 (1971).
61. *Town of Huntington v. Marsh* 859 F. 2d 1134 (1988).
62. *Animal Lovers Volunteers Association v. Cheney*, 795 F. Supp. 991 (1992).
63. *NORML v. Dept. of State*, 452 F. Supp. 1226 (1978).
64. *Citizens Organized to Protect the Environment v. Volpe*, 353 F. Supp. 520 (1972).
65. *Hiram Clarke Civic Club v. Lynn* 476 F. 2d Supp. 840 (1992).
66. *Miron v. Menominee County*, 795 F. Supp. 1226 (1978).
67. *Calipatria Land Co. v. Lujan*, 793 F. Supp. 241 (1990).
68. *Carol Van Strum v. John C. Lawn*, 1991 U.S. Lexis 3719 (1991).
69. 40 C.F.R. Sec. 1502.2 (d).
70. *Vermont Yankee Nuclear Power Corp. v. NRDC*, 435 U.S. 519, 98 S. Ct. 1197; *Robertson v. Methow Valley Citizens Council*, 490 U.S. 332, 109 S. Ct. 1835.
71. *Robertson*, 351.

72. CEQ 1978 Regulations, Section 1500.2 (f), available at http://ceq.eh.doe.gov/nepa/regs/ceq/toc_ceq.htm
73. 43 *Federal Register*, 55990, November 28, 1978.
74. R. Andrews, *Environmental Policy*,
75. Lettie M. Wenner, "Environmental Policy in the Courts," in *Environmental Policy in the 1990s*, ed. Norman J. Vig and Michael E. Kraft, 200.

Chapter 7

1. Mark Sagoff, "NEPA: Ethics, Economics, and Science in Environmental Law," in *Law of Environmental Protection*, ed. Sheldon Novick, Donald Stever, and Margaret Mellon.
2. Robert V. Bartlett, "Ecological Rationality: Reason and Environmental Policy," *Environmental Ethics* 8 (fall 1986): 229.
3. Caldwell, "NEPA Revisited," 22.
4. For a discussion on how NEPA has changed the organization outcomes and outputs of the U.S. Army Corps of Engineers, see Daniel A. Mazmanian and Jeanne Nienaber's *Can Organizations Change? Environmental Protection, Citizen Participation, and the Corps of Engineers*, and Serge Taylor's analysis of NEPA and the Forest Service in *Making Bureaucracies Think*.
5. Lynton Caldwell, introduction to Richard N. L. Andrews, *Environmental Policy and Administrative Change*.
6. Lynton Caldwell, "Analysis-Assessment-Decision: The Anatomy of Rational Policymaking," *Impact Assessment Bulletin* 9 (1991): 82.
7. See especially Taylor, *Making Bureaucracies Think*; Walter A. Rosenbaum, "The Bureaucracy and Environmental Policy," in *Environmental Politics and Policy: Theories and Evidence*; James P. Lester, ed., *Environmental Politics and Policy: Theories and Evidence*.
8. Lester B. Lave, *The Strategy of Social Regulation: Decision Frameworks for Policy*; Taylor, *Making Bureaucracies Think*, 359.
9. Lynton Caldwell, *A Study of Ways to Improve the Scientific Content and Methodology of Environmental Impact Analysis*; Caldwell, personal communication, September 8, 1994. While this is the only day cited, regular communication has been maintained over the years.
10. See Caldwell, "NEPA Revisited," 1989.
11. Caldwell, "Beyond NEPA"; italics in the original.
12. Philip M. Ferester, "Revitalizing the National Environmental Policy Act: Substantive Law Adaptations from NEPA's Progeny," *Harvard Environmental Law Review* 16 (1992): 257.
13. Council on Environmental Quality, *The National Environmental Policy Act: A Study of Its Effectiveness after Twenty-Five Years*, 33.
14. Vig and Kraft, *Environmental Policy for the 1990s*, 379.

15. Edward Walsh, "Staff Cut of 145 Said Proposed for White House," *Washington Post*, July 7, 1977, A1; "Backers of Environmental Unit Ask Carter to Keep It Intact," *Washington Post*, July 8, 1977, A3.

16. Executive Office of the President, Office of Management and Budget, Budget of the United States Government, Fiscal Year 1982, and Fiscal Year 1987.

17. Dinah Bear, Memo to Lynton Caldwell, December 4, 2000.

18. Norman J. Vig and Michael E. Kraft, *Environmental Policy in the 1990s*, 379.

19. John H. Cushman Jr., "A Clinton Cutback Upsets Environmentalists," *New York Times*, September 26, 1993, A1; Tom Kenworthy, "Clinton Plan on CEQ Sparks Tiff with Environmentalists," *Washington Post*, March 25, 1993, A22.

20. Senate Committee on Environment and Public Works, "Abolishing the Council on Environmental Quality." According to Dinah Bear, the Minerals Policy Center, the Center for Marine Conservation, and the Humane Society all opposed the elimination of the CEQ by President Clinton.

21. See Dreyfus and Ingram, "The National Environmental Policy Act," 243–62.

22. Professor Sally K. Fairfax is one exception to those who sing NEPA's praises. See especially, "A Disaster in the Environmental Movement: The National Environmental Policy Act has Wasted Environmentalists' Resources on Processing Papers," *Science* 743 (February 17, 1978): 199.

23. Council on Environmental Quality, *The National Environmental Policy Act*, iii.

24. Geoffrey Wandesforde-Smith, "Environmental Impact Assessment, Entrepreneurship, and Policy Change," in *Policy through Impact Assessment: Institutionalized Analysis as a Policy Strategy*, 155–66.

25. William V. Kennedy, "Environmental Impact Assessment in North America, Western Europe: What Has Worked Where, How, and Why," *International Environmental Reporter* 11 (April 13, 1988): 262; Council on Environmental Quality, 1996 Annual Report, 11.

26. Ray Clark, "The National Environmental Policy Act and the Role of the President's Council on Environmental Quality," quoted in Robert V. Bartlett, "Integrated Impact Assessment: The New Zealand Experiment," in *Environmental Policy: Transnational Issues and National Trends*, 160.

27. 40 C.F.R. Sec. 1502.7 (1990).

28. See Ray Clark and Larry Canter, eds. *Environmental Policy and NEPA: Past, Present, and Future*. See also, Elisabeth A. Blaug, "Use of the Environmental Assessment by Federal Agencies in NEPA Implementation."

29. Ray Clark, "The National Environmental Policy Act and the Role of the President's Council on Environmental Quality," *Environmental Professional* 15 (1): 4; Joseph Sax, "The (Unhappy) Truth about NEPA," *Oklahoma Law Review* 26 (1973): 239–48.

30. Environmental Protection Agency, *Guidelines for Carcinogenic Risk Assessment*, 993.

31. A. S. Wilkey and H. Arcain, "Social Impact Assessment under NEPA: The State of the Field," *Western Sociological Review* 8 (1997): 105–108.

32. W. R. Freudenburg, and K. N. Keating, "Applying Sociology to Policy: Social Science and the Environmental Impact Statement," *Rural Sociology* 50 (1985): 578–605.

33. C.F.R. Sec. 1504.14 (1989).

34. Frank Vanclay and Daniel A. Bronstein, *Environmental and Social Impact Assessment*, 32, 34.

35. Bear, "NEPA: Substance or Merely Process?" 85–88.

36. Vanclay and Bronstein, *Environmental and Social Impact Assessment*, 36.

37. 59 *Federal Register* 7629 (1994).

38. Council on Environmental Quality, Executive Office of the President, "Environmental Justice Guidance Under the National Environmental Policy Act," December 10, 1997. Available at http://ceq.eh.doe.gov/nepa/regs/guidance.html. Accessed on January 8, 2001. See also Melany Earnhardt, "Using the National Environmental Policy Act to Address Environmental Issues."

39. Ferester, "Revitalizing the National Environmental Policy Act," 269; Christopher Wood, *Environmental Impact Assessment: A Comparative Review*, 290.

40. 115 *Congressional Record* 40,416 (1969) (statement by Senator Jackson).

41. Available at http://www.whitehouse.gov/CEQ/About.html.

42. Caldwell, *The National Environmental Policy Act: An Agenda for the Future*, 98.

43. Ibid.

BIBLIOGRAPHY

Albert, Lee A. "Standing to Challenge Administrative Action: An Inadequate Surrogate for Claim for Relief." *Yale Law Journal* 83, no. 3 (1974): 425–27.

Allison, Graham. *Essence of Decision: Explaining the Cuban Missile Crisis.* Boston: Little, Brown, 1971.

Amy, Douglas J. "Decision Techniques for Environmental Policy." In *Managing Leviathan: Environmental Politics and the Administrative State,* ed. Robert Paehlke and Douglas Torgerson, 59–79. Lewiston, N.Y.: Broadview Press, 1990.

Anderson, Frederick R. *NEPA in the Courts: A Legal Analysis of the National Environmental Policy Act.* Baltimore: Johns Hopkins University Press, 1973.

Anderson, Frederick R., Daniel R. Mandelker, and A. Don Tarlock. *Environmental Protection: Law and Policy.* New York: Little, Brown, 1984.

Anderson, James E. *Public Policy-Making.* 3d ed. New York: Holt, Rinehart, and Winston, 1984.

Andrews, Richard N. L. "Agency Responses to NEPA: A Comparison and Implications." *Natural Resources Journal* 16 (2): 301–22.

———. *Environmental Policy and Administrative Change: Implementation of the National Environmental Policy Act.* Lexington, Mass.: Lexington Books, 1976.

———. "NEPA in Practice: Environmental Policy or Administrative Reform?" *Environmental Law Reporter* 6 (3): 50001–50009.

Ayton, Maureen W. *Environmental Quality: Selected Bills and Resolutions.* Washington, D.C.: Library of Congress Legislative Reference Service, Science Policy Research Division, June 20, 1968.

Baltimore Gas and Electric Co. v. Natural Resources Defense Council, Inc. 462 U.S. 87 (1983).

Bardach, Eugene. "On Designing Implementable Programs." In *Pitfalls of Analysis,* ed. G. Majone and E. Quade. New York: Wiley, 1979.

Bardach, Eugene, and Lucien Pugliaresi. "The Environmental Impact Statement vs. the Real World." *Public Interest* (fall 1977): 22–39.

Barfield, Claude, and Richard Corrigan. "Environmental Report/White House Seeks to Restrict Scope of Environmental Law." *National Journal* 4 (February 26, 1972): 336–49.

Bartlett, Robert V. "Ecological Rationality: Reason and Environmental Policy." *Environmental Ethics* 8 (fall 1986): 221–39.

———. "Ecological Reason in Administration: Environmental Impact Assessment and Administrative Theory." In *Managing Leviathan: Environmental Politics and the Administrative State,* ed. Robert Paehlke and Douglas Torgerson, 241. Lewiston, N.Y.: Broadview Press, 1990.

———. "Integrated Impact Assessment: The New Zealand Experiment." In *Environmental Policy: Transitional Issues and National Trends,* ed. Lynton Caldwell and Robert V. Bartlett, 160. Westport, Conn.: Quorum Books, 1997.

———. "The Rationality and Logic of NEPA Revisited." In *Environmental Policy and NEPA: Past, Present, and Future,* ed. Ray Clark and Larry W. Canter. Delray Beach, Fla.: St. Lucie Press, 1997.

———. "Rationality and the Logic of the National Environmental Policy Act." *Environmental Professional* 8 (1986):105–11.

———, ed. *Policy through Impact Assessment: Institutionalized Analysis as a Policy Strategy.* New York: Greenwood Press.

Bear, Dinah. "The National Environmental Policy Act." *Intergovernmental Perspectives* (summer 1992): 18.

———. "The National Environmental Quality Act: Its Origins and Evolution." *Natural Resources and the Environment* (fall 1995): 3–6, 69–73.

———. "NEPA: Substance or Merely Process?" *Forum for Applied Research and Public Policy* (summer 1993): 85–88.

Berger, Raoul. "Standing to Sue in Public Actions: Is It a Constitutional Requirement?" *Yale Law Journal* 78 (1969): 816.

Bernstein, Marver. *Regulating Business by Independent Commission.* Princeton, N.J.: Princeton University Press, 1955.

Blaug, Elisabeth A. "Use of the Environmental Assessment by Federal Agencies in NEPA Implementation." *Environmental Professional* 15 (1993): 57–65.

Blomquist, Robert F. "Supplemental Environmental Impact Statements under NEPA: A Conceptual Synthesis and Critique of Existing Legal Approaches to Environmental and Technological Changes." *Temple Environmental Law and Technology Journal* 8 (fall 1989): 1–54.

Bobrow, Davis B., and John S. Dryzek. *Policy Analysis by Design.* Pittsburgh: University of Pittsburgh Press, 1987.

Boggs, James P. "Procedural vs. Substantive in NEPA Law: Cutting the Gordian Knot." *Environmental Professional* 15 (1993): 30.

Brush, Bart. "National Environmental Policy Act." *Environmental Law* 22 (1992): 1963–67.

Buck, Susan J. *Understanding Environmental Administration and Law.* Washington, D.C.: Island Press, 1991.

Caldwell, Lynton K. "Achieving the NEPA Intent: New Directions in Politics, Science, and Law." In *Environmental Analysis: The NEPA Experience,* ed. Stephen G. Hildebrand and Johnnie B. Cannon. Boca Raton, Fla.: Lewis Publishers, CRC Press, 1993.

———. "Analysis—Assessment—Decision: The Anatomy of Rational Policy-making." *Impact Assessment Bulletin* 9 (1991): 81–92.

———. "Beyond NEPA: Future Significance of the National Environmental Policy Act." *Harvard Environmental Law Review* 22, no. 2032, 203.

———. "The Ecosystem as a Criterion for Public Land Policy." *Natural Resources Journal* 10 (2): 203–21.

———. *Environment: A Challenge to Modern Society.* New York: Doubleday, 1971.

———. "Environment: A New Focus for Public Policy?" *Public Administration Review* 23 (1963): 132–39.

———. "The Environmental Impact Statement: A Misused Tool." In *Environmental Impact Analysis,* ed. Ravinder Jain and Bruce Hutchings. Urbana: University of Illinois Press, 1978.

———. "Environmental Policy in a Hypertrophic Society." *Natural Resources Journal* 11 (July 1971): 417–26.

———. Introduction to *Environmental Policy and Administrative Change,* by Richard N. L. Andrews. Lexington, Mass.: Lexington Books, 1976.

———. "Is NEPA Inherently Self-Defeating?" *Environmental Law Reporter* 9 (1979): 50001–50007.

———. "The National Environmental Policy Act: Retrospective and Prospect." *Environmental Law Reporter* 6 (3): 50030–38.

———. "The National Environmental Policy Act: An Agenda for the Future." Bloomington: Indiana University Press, 1998.

———. "NEPA at Twenty: A Retrospective Critique." *Natural Resources and Environment* 5 (1): 6–8, 49–50.

———. "NEPA Revisited: A Call for a Constitutional Amendment." *Environmental Forum* 6 (1989): 17–22.

———. "Restructuring for Coordinative Policy and Action." *Public Administration Review* 28 (1968): 301–303.

———. *Science and the National Environmental Policy Act: Redirecting Policy through Procedural Reform.* University: University of Alabama Press, 1982.

———. *A Study of Ways to Improve the Scientific Content and Methodology of Environmental Impact Analysis.* Final Report to the National Science Foundation on Grant PRA-79-10014. Bloomington: Indiana University School of Public and Environmental Affairs, 1982.

———. "Understanding Impact Analysis: Technical Process, Administrative Reform, Policy Principle." In *Policy through Impact Assessment: Institutional Analysis as a Policy Strategy,* ed. Robert V. Bartlett. Westport, Conn.: Greenwood Press, 1989.

Caldwell, Lynton K., and Robert V. Bartlett, eds. *Environmental Policy: Transnational Issues and Environmental Trends.* Westport, Conn.: Quorum Books, 1997.

Caldwell, Lynton, with William J. Van Ness. *A National Policy for the Environment.* Special report to the Senate Committee on Interior and Insular Affairs, 90th Congress, 2d sess., July 11, 1968.

Calvert Cliffs' Coordinating Committee v. Atomic Energy Commission, 449 F. 2d 1109 (D.C. Cir. 1971), cert. denied, 404 U.S. 942 (1972).

Citizens to Preserve Overton Park v. Volpe, 309 F. Supp. 1189 (W.D. Tenn), affirmed, 432 F. 2d 1307 (6th Cir. 1970), revised, 401 U.S. 402 (1972).

Carlson, Cynthia. "NEPA and the Conservation of Biological Diversity." *Environmental Law* 19 (1988): 15–36.

Carson, Rachel. *Silent Spring.* New York: Houghton, Mifflin, 1962.

Clark, Jeanne N., and Daniel McCool. *Staking Out the Terrain: Power Differentials among Natural Resource Management Agencies.* Albany: State University of New York Press, 1985.

Clark, Ray. "The National Environmental Policy Act and the Role of the President's Council on Environmental Quality." *Environmental Professional* 15 (1): 4–6.

Clark, Ray, and Larry W. Canter, eds. *Environmental Policy and NEPA: Past, Present, and Future.* Saint Lucie, Fla.: Saint Lucie Press, 1997.

Commission on Federal Paperwork. *Environmental Impact Statements.* Washington, D.C.: U.S. Government Printing Office, 1977.

Commoner, Barry. *The Closing Circle.* New York: Knopf, 1971.

Comptroller General of the United States. *The Council on Environmental Quality: A Tool in Shaping National Policy.* U.S. Printing Office, March 18, 1981.

———. *Environmental Assessment Efforts for Proposed Projects Have Been Ineffective.* Report no. RED-75–393. Washington, D.C.: U.S. Government Printing Office, 1975.

———. *The Environmental Impact Statement—It Seldom Causes Long Project Delays But Could Be More Useful If Prepared Earlier.* Report no. CED-77–79. Washington, D.C.: U.S. Government Printing Office, 1977.

Congressional Quarterly Almanac. (1969): 513, 525, 527.

Congressional Record. 91st Congress, 1st Sess., 1969. Vol. 39, pt. 702, 40416–18.

———. 91st Congress, 1st Sess., 1969. Vol. 115, pts. 11, 14, 21.

Congressional White Paper on a National Policy for the Environment. Special report to the U.S. Senate Committee on Interior and Insular Affairs. Washington, D.C.: U.S. Government Printing Office, 1968.

Cooley, Richard A., and Geoffrey Wandesforde-Smith. *Congress and the Environment.* Seattle: University of Washington Press, 1970.

Corps of Engineers. *Effect of NEPA on the Corps Studies and Projects, 1970–1978.* Washington, D.C.: Chief of Engineers, HQDA (DAEN-CWRO- P), 1979.

Cortner, Hanna. "A Case Analysis of Policy Implementation: The National Environmental Policy Act of 1969." *Natural Resources Journal* 16 (1976): 323–38.

Council on Environmental Quality. *Environmental Impact Statements: An Analysis of Six Years' Experience by Seventy Federal Agencies.* Washington, D.C.: U.S. Government Printing Office, 1976.

———. Environmental Quality. Annual Report. Washington, D.C.: U.S. Government Printing Office, 1991.

———. Environmental Quality. Annual Report. Washington, D.C.: U.S. Government Printing Office, 1993.

————. Environmental Quality. Annual Report. Washington, D.C.: U.S. Government Printing Office, 1994.

————. Environmental Quality. Annual Report. Washington, D.C.: U.S. Government Printing Office, 1996.

————. Environmental Quality. Annual Report. Washington, D.C.: U.S. Government Printing Office, 1997.

————. *Environmental Quality: Twenty-Second Annual Report*, March 1992.

————. "Guidelines." 36 *Federal Register* 7724–29 (April 23, 1971). ELR 46049.

————. *The National Environmental Policy Act: A Study of Its Effectiveness after Twenty-Five Years.* Washington, D.C., January 1997.

————. *NEPA: Today's Law for the Future—Proceedings of CEQ/EPA Conference at the State Department, September 21–22, 1989.* Washington, D.C.: Council on Environmental Quality, 1989.

————. *A Report to the Council of Environmental Quality, Executive Office of the President.* Environmental Law Institute. Washington, D.C.: U.S. Government Printing Office, 1981.

Culhane, Paul J. "The Effectiveness of NEPA." Letter. *Science* 202: 1035–36.

————. "Natural Resource Policy: Procedural Change and Substantive Environmentalism." In *Nationalizing Government*, ed. Theodore Lowi and Alan Stone. Beverly Hills: Sage Publications, 1978.

————. "NEPA's Effect on Agency Decision Making." *Environmental Law* 20 (1990): 681–702.

————. *Public Lands Politics.* Baltimore: Johns Hopkins University Press, 1981.

Culhane, Paul J., and Paul H. Friesema. "Environmental Impact Statements and Research on Public Policy and Applied Sciences." In *EIS Annual Review 1*, ed. Ned J. Cronin. Washington, D.C.: Information Resources Press, 1978.

————. "Social Impacts, Politics, and the Environmental Impact Statement Process." *Natural Resources Journal* 16 (1976): 339–56.

Culhane, Paul J., Paul H. Friesema, and Janice A. Beecher. *Forecasts and Environmental Decisionmaking: The Content and Predictive Accuracy of Environmental Impact Statements.* Boulder, Colo.: Westview Press, 1987.

Cushman, John H., Jr. "A Clinton Cutback Upsets Environmentalists." *New York Times*, September 26, 1993, A1.

Daneke, Gregory A. "Whither Environmental Regulation?" *Journal of Public Policy* 4 (2): 139–51.

Davis, Kenneth C. *Administrative Law.* St. Paul, Minn.: West Publishing, 1951.

Davis, Robert. "Do We Exalt EIS Form over Substance?" In *Environmental Impact Assessment: Proceedings of a Conference on the Preparation and Review of Environmental Impact Statements*, ed. Nicolas A. Robinson, 203. Albany: New York State Bar Association, 1989.

Downs, Anthony. *Inside Bureaucracy.* Boston: Little, Brown, 1967.

————. "Up and Down with Ecology—The 'Issue-Attention Cycle.'" *Public Interest* (summer 1972): 38–50.

Dreyfus, Daniel A., and Helen M. Ingram. "The National Environmental Policy Act: A View of Intent and Practice." *National Resources Journal* 16 (2): 243–62.

Dubos, René. *The Fitness of Man's Environment, Smithsonian Annual 2.* New York: Harper and Row, 1968.

———. *Reason Awake: Science for Man.* New York: Columbia University Press, 1970.

Duke Power Co. v. Carolina Environmental Study Group, Inc. 438 U.S. 59, 73–74, 1978.

Dunlap, Riley E., and Angela G. Mertig, eds. *American Environmentalism: The U.S. Environmental Movement 1970–1990.* Washington, D.C.: Taylor and Francis, 1992.

Dunster, Julian. "Assessing the Sustainability of Canadian Forest Management: Progress or Procrastination?" *Environmental Impact Assessment Review* 12 (1992): 67–84.

Earnhardt, Melany. "Using the National Environmental Policy Act to Address Environmental Justice Issues." *Clearinghouse Review* (special issue 1995): 436–45.

Easton, David. *A Systems Analysis of Political Life.* New York: Wiley, 1965.

Ehrlich, Paul R. *The Population Bomb.* New York: Ballantine, 1968.

Ehrlich, Paul R., and Anne H. Ehrlich. *Betrayal of Science and Reason: How Anti-Environmental Rhetoric Threatens Our Future.* Washington, D.C.: Island Press, 1998.

Endangered Species Act. 11(g), 116 U.S.C. 1540 (g), 1988.

Ernsdorff, Gary M. "The Agency for International Development and NEPA: A Duty Unfulfilled." *Washington Law Review* 67 (January 1992): 133–54.

Executive Order no. 11, 472. President Richard M. Nixon. White House. Washington, D.C., 1969.

Executive Order no. 11514, 35 *Federal Register* 4247 (1970).

Executive Order no. 11991, 42 *Federal Register* 26, 967 (1977).

Executive Order no. 55994, 43 *Federal Register* Sec. 1502.1 (November 29, 1978).

Eyestone, Robert. *From Social Issues to Public Policy.* New York: Wiley, 1978.

Fairfax, Sally. "A Disaster in the Environmental Movement." *Science* 199 (17): 743–48.

———. "The Effectiveness of NEPA." Letter. *Science* 202: 1038–40.

Ferester, Philip M. "Revitalizing the National Environmental Policy Act: Substantive Law Adaptations from NEPA's Progeny." *Harvard Environmental Law Review* 16 (1992): 207–69.

Feyerabend, Paul. *Science in a Free Society.* London: NLB, 1978.

Findley, Roger W., and Daniel Farber. *Environmental Law in a Nutshell.* St. Paul, Minn.: West Publishing, 1991.

Finn, Terrence. "Conflict and Compromise: Congress Makes a Law, The Passage of the National Environmental Policy Act." Ph.D. diss., Georgetown University, 1972.

Firestone, David B., and Frank C. Reed. *Environmental Law for Non-Lawyers.* South Royalton, Vt.: SoRo Press, 1993.

Fletcher, William A. "The Structure of Standing." *Yale Law Journal* 98, no. 2 (1988): 221–91.

Fogleman, Valerie M. *Guide to the National Environmental Policy Act: Interpretations, Applications, and Compliance.* New York: Quorum Books, 1990.

French, Susannah T. "Judicial Review of the Administrative Record in NEPA Litigation." *California Law Review* 81 (1993): 929–90.

Freudenburg, W. R., and K. N. Keating. "Applying Sociology to Policy: Social Science and the Environmental Impact Statement." *Rural Sociology* 50 (1985): 578–605.

Frost, Don J. "*Amoco Production Co. v. Village of Gambel and Motor Vehicle Manufacturers Association v. State Farm Mutual Automobile Insurance Co.*: Authority Warranting Reconsideration of the Substantive Goals of the National Environmental Policy Act." *Alaska Law Review* 5 (1): 15–67.

Fuller, Buckminster. *Operating Manual for Spaceship Earth.* New York: Pocket Books, 1970.

Gerston, Larry N., Cynthia Fraleigh, and Robert Schwab. *The Deregulated Society.* Belmont, Mass.: Wadsworth, 1988.

Gillette, Robert. "National Environmental Policy Act: Signs of Backlash Are Evident." *Science* 176: 301.

Gilpin, Alan. *Environmental Impact Assessment (EIA): Cutting Edge for the Twenty-First Century.* Cambridge: Cambridge University Press, 1995.

Goldsmith, and Banks. "Environmental Values: Institutional Responsibility and the Supreme Court." *Harvard Environmental Law Review* 7 (1983): 5–6.

Hammond, Kenneth R., ed. *Judgment and Decision in Public Policy Formation.* Boulder, Colo.: Westview Press, American Association for the Advancement of Science, 1978.

Hanley v. Kleindienst. 471 F. 2d 823, 831, 1972.

Hanley v. Mitchell. 460 F. 2d 640 (2D Cir.) cert. denied, 409 U.S. 990, 1972.

Hansen, James. "Law Doesn't Accomplish Its Goals." *Roll Call*, April 19, 1999, 9–10.

Hardin, Garrett. "The Tragedy of the Commons." *Science* 162: 1243–1248.

Harnick, Peter. "Testing the Movement: It's Time to Save NEPA." *Environmental Action* 3 (April 15): 3.

Hartmann, Clay. "NEPA: Business as Usual: The Weakness of the National Environmental Policy Act." *Journal of Air Law and Commerce* 55 (3): 709–61.

Hays, Samuel P. *Beauty, Health, and Permanence: Environmental Politics in the United States, 1955–1985.* Cambridge: Cambridge University Press, 1987.

———. *Conservation and the Gospel of Efficiency: The Progressive Conservatism Movement, 1890–1920.* Pittsburgh: University of Pittsburgh Press, 1999.

Hill, William W. "NEPA's Effect on the Consideration of Alternatives: A Crucial Test." *Natural Resources Journal* 18 (2): 285–312.

Hill, William W., and Leonard Ortolano. "Effects of NEPA's Review and Comment Process on Water Resource Planning." *Water Resources Research* 12 (1976): 1039–99.

Inglehart, Ronald. *The Silent Revolution: Changing Values and Political Styles among Western Publics.* Princeton, N.J.: Princeton University Press, 1977.

Ingram, Helen, and Scott J. Ullery. "Public Participation in Environmental Decision

Making: Substance or Illusion." In *Public Participation in Planning*, ed. F. T. Koppock and W. R. D. Sewell. New York: Wiley, 1977.

Jaffe, Louis L. "Standing to Secure Judicial Review: Private Actions." *Harvard Law Review* 75 (1961): 255.

———."Standing to Secure Judicial Review: Public Actions." *Harvard Law Review* 74 (1961): 1265–1314.

Janis, Irving L. *Victims of Groupthink: A Psychological Study of Foreign-Policy Decisions and Fiascoes.* Boston: Houghton, Mifflin, 1972.

Jones, Charles O. *An Introduction to the Study of Public Policy.* 2d ed. Boston: Duxbury Publishing, 1977.

Kennedy, William V. "Environmental Impact Assessment in North America, Western Europe: What Has Worked Where, How, and Why." *International Environmental Reporter* 11 (April 13, 1988): 262.

Kenworthy, Tom. "Clinton Plan on CEQ Sparks Tiff with Environmentalists." *Washington Post,* March 25, 1993, A22.

Kingdon, John. *Agendas, Alternatives, and Public Policies.* Boston: Little Brown, 1984.

Kreske, Diori L. *Environmental Impact Statements: A Practical Guide for Agencies, Citizens, and Consultants.* New York: Wiley, 1996.

Lake Erie Alliance for Protection of Coastal Corridor v. Corps of Engineers. 486 F. Supp. 707, 710–14, 1980.

Lave, Lester B. *The Strategy of Social Regulation: Decision Frameworks for Policy.* Washington, D.C.: Brookings Institution, 1981.

Lazear, Robert. *The National Environmental Policy Act and Its Implementation: A Selected, Annotated Bibliography.* Madison: Wisconsin Seminars on Resource and Environmental Systems, Institute for Environmental Studies, University of Wisconsin, 1978.

Leopold, Aldo. *A Sand County Almanac.* New York: Oxford University Press, 1968.

Lester, James P., and Joseph Stewart, Jr. *Public Policy: An Evolutionary Approach.* Belmont, Calif.: Wadsworth-Thompson Learning, 2000.

———, ed. *Environmental Politics and Policy: Theories and Evidence.* 2d ed. Durham, N.C.: Duke University Press, 1995.

Lindblom, Charles. *The Intelligence of Democracy.* New York: Free Press, 1965.

———. *The Policy-Making Process.* Englewood Cliffs, N.J.: Prentice-Hall, 1968.

———. "The Science of 'Muddling Through.'" *Public Administration Review* 19 (spring 1959): 79–88.

Lindstrom, Matthew J. "The Withering Away of NEPA's Substantive Law." *Journal of Land, Resources, and Environmental Law* 20, no. 2 (2000).

Lindstrom, Matthew J., and Martin A. Nie. "Public Participation and Agency." *The Public Manager* 29, no. 1 (Spring 2000).

———. *Public Participation in Transportation Planning.* Grant no. SPR-PL-1-(49) 452. Springfield, Va.: National Technical Information Service, 1996.

Liroff, Richard. "The Effectiveness of NEPA." Letter. *Science* 202 (4372): 1036–38.

————. "Environmental Administration: NEPA and Federal Agencies." In *Environmental Politics,* ed. Stuart S. Nagel. New York: Praeger, 1974.

————. *The Environmental Impact Statement Process under NEPA.* Washington, D.C.: Environmental Law Institute, 1978.

————. *A National Policy for the Environment: NEPA and Its Aftermath.* Bloomington: Indiana University Press, 1976.

————. "NEPA—Where Have We Been and Where Are We Going?" *American Planning Association Journal* (April 1980): 154–61.

————. "Oil vs. Oysters—Lessons for Environmental Regulation of Industrial Siting from the Hampton Roads Refinery Controversy." *Boston College Environmental Affairs Law Review* 11 (fall 1984): 705.

————. Ph.D. diss., Indiana University, 1975.

Lowi, Theodore. "American Business, Public Policy, and Political Theory." *World Politics* 16 (1964): 677–715.

Lujan v. Defenders of Wildlife. 112 S. Ct. 2130, 1992.

Lujan v. National Wildlife Federation. 110 S. Ct. 3177, 1990.

Majone, Giandomenico, and Aaron Wildavsky. "Implementation as Evolution." In *Implementation: How Great Expectations in Washington Are Dashed in Oakland,* eds. Jeffrey L. Pressman and Aaron Wildavsky. Berkeley: University of California Press, 1984.

Malik, Madhu, and Robert V. Bartlett. "Formal Guidance for the Use of Science in EIA: Analysis of Agency Procedures for Implementing NEPA." *Environmental Professional* 15 (1993): 34–45.

Mandelker, Daniel. *Environment and Equity: A Regulatory Challenge.* New York: McGraw-Hill, 1981.

————. *NEPA Law and Litigation: The National Environmental Policy Act.* Wilmette, Ill.: Callaghan, 1984.

Marsh v. Oregon Natural Resources Council. 109 S. Ct. 1851, 1989.

Martin, Brian. "Anarchist Science Policy." *Raven* 7, no. 2 (summer 1994): 140–41.

Mazmanian, Daniel A., and Jeanne Nienaber. *Can Organizations Change? Environmental Protection, Citizen Participation, and the Corps of Engineers.* Washington, D.C.: Brookings Institution, 1979.

McCool, Daniel. *Command of the Waters: Iron Triangles, Federal Water Development, and Indian Water.* Berkeley: University of California Press, 1987. Reprint, Tucson: University of Arizona Press, 1994.

McElfish, James, and Elissa Parker. *Rediscovering the National Environmental Policy Act: Back to the Future.* Washington, D.C.: Environmental Law Institute, 1995.

McHarg, Ian L. *Design with Nature.* Garden City, N.Y.: American Museum of Natural History, Natural History Press, 1969.

Meier, Kenneth J. *Politics and the Bureaucracy: Policymaking in the Fourth Branch of Government.* Belmont, Calif.: Wadsworth, 1993.

Metropolitan Edison Co. v. People Against Nuclear Energy. 460 U.S. 766, 1983.

Miller, Alan, et al. "The National Environmental Policy Act and Agency Policy Making: Neither Paper Tiger nor Straightjacket." *Environmental Law Reporter* 6 (3): 5020–29.

Minnesota Public Interest Research Group v. Butz. 498 F. 2d 1314, 1320, 1974.

Moe, Terry. "The Politics of Structured Choice: Toward a Theory of Public Bureaucracy." In *Organizational Theory: From Chester Barnard to the Present and Beyond,* ed. Oliver Williamson. New York: Oxford University Press, 1990.

Moe, Terry, and Scott Wilson. "Presidents and the Politics of Structure." *Law and Contemporary Problems* 57 (1994): 1–44.

Moore, John E. "Recycling the Regulatory Agencies." *Public Administration Review* (July–August 1972): 291–98.

Multiple Use—Sustained Yield Act of 1960. 16 U.S.C. secs. 528 and 531.

NAACP v. Medical Center, Inc. 584 F. 2d 619, 626–27, 634 (3d Cir.), 1972.

Nagel, Stuart S. *Environmental Politics.* New York: Praeger, 1974.

National Environmental Policy Act of 1969. Public law no. 91–190, 42 U.S.C. 4321–61, 1969.

National Helium Corp. v. Morton. 455 F. 2d 650, 655 (10th Cir.), 1971.

Niskanen, William. *Bureaucracy and Representative Government.* Chicago: Aldine, 1971.

"Nixon Promises an Urgent Fight to End Pollution." *New York Times,* January 2, 1970, A1.

O'Brien, Mary H. "NEPA as It Was Meant to Be: *NAACP v. Block, Herbicides, and Region 6 Forest Service.*" *Environmental Law* 20 (1990): 735–45.

O'Riordan, Timothy. *Environmentalism.* London: Pion, 1976.

Orloff, Neil, and George Brooks. *The National Environmental Policy Act: Cases and Materials.* Washington, D.C.: Bureau of National Affairs, 1980.

Ortolano, et al. *Environmental Considerations in Three Infrastructure Planning Agencies: An Overview of Research Findings.* Report IPM-6. Palo Alto, Calif.: Stanford University Department of Civil Engineering, 1978.

Ozawa, Connie. "Targeting the NEPA Process." *Environmental Impact Assessment Review* 3 (1): 102–108.

Pallone, Frank. "Thirty Years of NEPA: It Works in My State." *Roll Call,* April 19, 1999, 9.

Plater, Zygmunt J. B., Robert Adams, and William Goldfarb. *Environmental Law and Policy: Nature, Law, and Society.* St. Paul, Minn.: West Publishing Co., 1992.

Public Papers of the President, Richard M. Nixon. Statement about the National Environmental Policy Act of 1969 (January 1, 1970).

Quirk, Paul. *Industry Influence in Federal Regulatory Agencies.* Princeton, N.J.: Princeton University Press, 1981.

Ripley, Randall, and Grace A. Franklin. *Congress, the Bureaucracy, and Public Policy.* Chicago: Nelson-Hall, 1985.

———. *Policy Implementation and Bureaucracy.* 2d ed. Chicago: Dorsey Press, 1986.

Robertson v. Methow Valley Citizens Council. 109 S. Ct. 1835, 1989.

Robison, Wade L. *Decisions in Doubt: The Environment and Public Policy.* Hanover, N.H.: University Press of New England, 1994.

Rochefort, David A., and Roger W. Cobb. *The Politics of Problem Definition: Shaping the Policy Agenda.* Lawrence: University of Kansas Press, 1994.

Rodgers, William H. *Environmental Law: Handbook Series.* 2d ed. St. Paul, Minn.: West Publishing, 1994.

Rose, Hilary, and Steven Rose, eds. *The Political Economy of Science.* London: Macmillan, 1976.

———. *The Radicalization of Science.* London: Macmillan, 1976.

Rosenbaum, Walter. "The Bureaucracy and Environmental Policy." In *Environmental Politics and Policy: Theories and Evidence,* ed. James P. Lester. 2d ed. Durham, N.C.: Duke University Press, 1995.

———. "The End of Illusion: NEPA and the Limits of Judicial Review." In *Environmental Politics,* ed. Stuart Nagel. New York: Praeger, 1974.

———. "Public Involvement as Reform and Ritual: The Development of Federal Participation Programs." In *Citizen Participation in America,* ed. Stuart Langton. Lexington, Mass.: Lexington Books, 1978.

Rosenthal, Alan. *The Third House: Lobbyists and Lobbying in the States.* Washington, D.C.: CQ Press, 1993.

Sabatier, Paul, and Daniel Mazmanian. *Effective Policy Implementation.* Lexington, Mass.: Heath, 1981.

———. *Implementation and Public Policy.* Chicago: Scott, Foresman, 1983.

———. "The Implementation of Public Policy: A Framework for Analysis." *Policy Studies Journal* 8 (1980): 538–60.

Sagoff, Mark. "NEPA: Ethics, Economics, and Science in Environmental Law." In *Law of Environmental Protection,* eds. Sheldon Novick, Donald Stever, and Margaret Mellon. Vol. 1. New York: Clark Boardman, 1987.

Sanera, Michael, and Jane S. Shaw. *Facts, Not Fear: A Parent's Guide to Teaching Children about the Environment.* Washington, D.C.: Regnery Publishing, 1996.

Sax, Joseph L. "The (Unhappy) Truth about NEPA." *Oklahoma Law Review* 26 (1973): 239–48.

Schachter, Esther R. "Standards for Evaluating a NEPA Environmental Statement." *Public Utilities Fortnightly* 90 (5): 29–32.

Schlager, Edella, and William Blomquist. "Field Essay: A Comparison of Three Emerging Theories of the Policy Process." *Political Research Quarterly* (spring 1996): 651–72.

Schneider, Mark, Paul Teske, and Michael Mintrom. *Public Entrepreneurs: Agents for Change in American Government.* Princeton, N.J.: Princeton University Press, 1995.

Scientists' Institute for Public Information, Inc. V.AEC, 481 F. 2nd 1079 (D.C. Cir. 1973).

SCRAP v. U.S. 346 F. Supp. 189, 201, 1972.

Shilton, David C. "Is the Supreme Court Hostile to NEPA? Some Possible Explanations for a 12–0 Record." *Environmental Law* 20, no. 3 (1990): 551–68.

Sierra Club v. Hodel. 848 F. 2d 661, 673 n. 15 (9th Cir.), 1975.

Simon, Julian L. *The Ultimate Resource.* Princeton, N.J.: Princeton University Press, 1981.

Smith, Zachary A. *The Environmental Policy Paradox.* 2d ed. Englewood Cliffs, N.J.: Prentice-Hall, 1995.

Squillace, Mark, and Karin P. Sheldon, eds. *The NEPA Litigation Guide.* Chicago: American Bar Association, Section of Natural Resources, Energy, and Environmental Law, 1999.

Stigler, George. "The Theory of Economic Regulation." *The Bell Journal of Economics and Management Science* 2 (spring 1971): 3–21.

Stryker's Bay Neighborhood Council v. Karlen. 100 S. Ct. 497, 1980.

Taylor, Serge. *Making Bureaucracies Think: The Environmental Impact Strategy of Administrative Reform.* Palo Alto, Calif.: Stanford University Press, 1984.

Theodoulou, Stella A., and Matthew A. Cahn. *Public Policy: The Essential Readings.* Englewood Cliffs, N.J.: Prentice-Hall, 1995.

Tilleman, William A. "Public Participation in the Environmental Impact Assessment Process: A Comparative Study of Impact Assessment in Canada, the United States, and the European Community." *Columbia Journal of Transnational Law* (1995): 337.

Toxic Substances Control Act. 20, 15 U.S.C. 2619, 1988.

Tzoumis, Kelly, and Linda Finegold. "Looking at the Quality of Draft Environmental Impact Statements in the United States over Time: Have Ratings Improved?" Typescript, 1999.

Udall, Stewart. *The Quiet Crisis.* Salt Lake City: Peregrine Smith, 1963.

U.S. Department of the Interior. *A Study of Bureau Organizational Arrangements for NEPA Compliance.* Washington, D.C.: Department of the Interior, Office of Administrative and Management Policy, 1978.

U.S. Environmental Protection Agency. *Guidelines for Carcinogenic Risk Assessment.* 51 *Federal Register* 33, 1986, 993.

U.S. House Committee on Merchant Marine and Fisheries. Subcommittee on Fisheries and Wildlife Conservation and the Environment. Hearings on H.R. 1113. 101st Congress, 1st sess., 1989.

———. Subcommittee on Fisheries and Wildlife Conservation and the Environment. Hearings on H.R. 6750, H.R. 11886, H.R. 11942, H.R. 12077, H.R. 12207, H.R. 12209, H.R. 12228, H.R. 12409. 91st Congress, 1st Sess., 1969.

U.S. House Committee on Science and Astronautics. Subcommittee on Science, Research, and Development. *Managing the Environment.* 90th Congress, 2d sess., 1969. Committee Print.

U.S. House-Senate Joint Colloquium to Discuss a National Policy for the Environment. 90th Congress, 2d sess., 1968.

U.S. Senate. *National Environmental Policy Act of 1969.* 91st Congress, 1st sess., 1969. Report 91–296.

U.S. Senate Committee on Environment and Public Works. "Abolishing the Council on Environmental Quality." Hearings on Section 112 of S.171. Termination of the Council on Environmental Quality and Transfer of Functions. 103d Congress, 1st sess., April 1, 1993, 36–38, 41, 45–46.

U.S. Senate Committee on Interior and Insular Affairs. Hearings on S. 1075, S. 237, and S. 1752. 92d Congress, 1st sess., April 16, 1969.

———. *National Environmental Policy Act of 1969.* Conference Report, *Congressional Record,* vol. 115, part. 30, 91st Congress, 1st sess.

USALSA Report: Environmental Law Division, "Note: Fourth Circuit Court Looks at NEPA Cost Benefit Analysis," *Army Lawyer* 38, June, 1999.

Vanclay, Frank, and Daniel A. Bronstein. *Environmental and Social Impact Assessment.* New York: Wiley, 1995.

Vermont Yankee Nuclear Power Co. v. Natural Resources Defense Council. 435 U.S. 519, 98 S. Ct. 1197, 55 L. Ed. 2d, 1978.

Vig, Norman J., and Michael E. Kraft, *Environmental Policy in the 1990s.* Washington, D.C.: Congressional Quarterly Press, 1990.

Vogel, David. *National Styles of Regulation: Environmental Policy in Great Britain and the United States.* Ithaca, N.Y.: Cornell University Press, 1986.

Walsh, Edward. "Backers of Environmental Unit Ask Carter to Keep It Intact." *Washington Post,* July 8, 1977, A3.

———. "Staff Cut of 145 Said Proposed for White House." *Washington Post,* July 7, 1977, A1.

Wandesforde-Smith, Geoffrey. "Environmental Impact Assessment, Entrepreneurship, and Policy Change." In *Policy through Impact Assessment: Institutionalized Analysis as a Policy Strategy,* ed. Robert V. Bartlett. Westport, Conn.: Greenwood Press, 1989.

———. "National Policy for the Environment: Politics and the Concept of Stewardship." In *Congress and the Environment,* eds. Richard A. Cooley and Geoffrey Wandesforde-Smith. Seattle: University of Washington Press, 1970.

Wandesforde-Smith, Geoffrey, et al. "Policy Impact Analysis and Environmental Management: Review and Comment." *Policy Studies Journal* 4 (1): 81–90.

Warm Springs Dam Task Force v. Gribble. 565 F. 2d 549 (9th Cir.), 1977.

Weiland, Paul S. "Amending the National Environmental Policy Act: Federal Environmental Protection in the Twenty-First Century." *Journal of Land Use and Environmental Law* (spring 1997).

Wenner, Lettie M. "Environmental Policy in the Courts." In *Environmental Policy in the 1990s,* eds. Norman J. Vig and Michael E. Kraft. Washington, D.C.: Congressional Quarterly Press, 1990.

———. *The Environmental Decade in Court.* Bloomington: Indiana University Press, 1982.

Whitaker, John. *Striking A Balance: Environment and Natural Resources Policy in the Nixon-Ford Years.* Washington, D.C.: American Enterprise Institute for Public Policy Research, 1976.

Wichelman, Allan F. "Administrative Implementation of the National Environmental Policy Act of 1969: A Conceptual Framework for Explaining Differential Response." *Natural Resources Journal* 16 (2): 263–300.

Wildavsky, Aaron. *Speaking Truth to Power: The Art and Craft of Policy Analysis.* Boston: Little, Brown, 1979.

Wilkey, A. S., and H. Arcain. "Social Impact Assessment under NEPA: The State of the Field." *Western Sociological Review* 8 (1997): 105–108.

Wilson, James Q. *The Politics of Regulation.* New York: Basic Books, 1980.

Wood, Christopher. *Environmental Impact Assessment: A Comparative Review.* Essex, Eng.: Longman, 1995.

Worsham, John P. *The National Environmental Policy Act and Related Matters: A Selected Bibliography.* Monticello, Ill.: Vance Bibliographies, 1978.

"Worst Case Analysis: A Continued Requirement under the National Environmental Policy Act?" *Columbia Journal of Environmental Law* 53 (1987): 60.

Yost, Nicholas C. "Forty Most Asked Questions Concerning CEQ's National Environmental Policy Act Regulations," reprinted in the *Federal Register* 46, no. 18026 (March 23, 1981) as amended.

———. *National Environmental Policy Act Regulations. A Memorandum for Federal NEPA Liaisons, Federal, State, and Local Officials, and Other Persons Involved in the NEPA Process.* Washington, D.C.: Council on Environmental Quality, 1981.

———. "NEPA's Promise—Partially Fulfilled." *Environmental Law* 20 (1990): 533–49.

———. "Scoping Guidance." A Memorandum for General Counsels, NEPA Liaisons, and Participants in Scoping. Washington, D.C.: Council on Environmental Quality, 1981.

INDEX

MATTHEW J. LINDSTROM, who earned his Ph.D. from Northern Arizona University, is an assistant professor in the Political Science Department and Environmental Studies Program at Siena College in Loudonville, New York. He is the author of several journal articles and is currently editing a book on suburban sprawl and eco-cities. In addition, he works as the director of Eco-Logic: Siena Institute for Sustainable Land Use.

ZACHARY A. SMITH earned his Ph.D. from the University of California, Santa Barbara, and is a professor at Northern Arizona University in Flagstaff. He has served as a consultant on environmental matters and is the author or editor of fifteen books and more than thirty articles on environmental policy topics.